CW01083466

Primary Sources, Historical Collections: A Guide to the Old Persian Inscriptions, with a foreword by T. S. Wentworth

Herbert Cushing Tolman

Preface

This book, from the series *Primary Sources: Historical Books of the World (Asia and Far East Collection)*, represents an important historical artifact on Asian history and culture. Its contents come from the legions of academic literature and research on the subject produced over the last several hundred years.

The seemingly singular subject of "Asia" is undoubtedly too broad for any single contributor, or even institution, to adequately articulate. The region is immense in size, the history spans several thousand years, and the culture is almost unimaginably broad. Moreover, Asia is not in and of itself a single area with fixed geographic boundaries, but rather covers many nations, empires, regions, tribes, ethnicities, religions, etc., all of which have changed and evolved over the past millennia due to conflicts, conquests, changing regimes, and the like. No one historian or researcher could adequately travel the continent in their lifetime, let alone become a subject matter expert on the wealth of knowledge that has been derived from the region.

Practically speaking, Asian history and culture do not encompass a single geography but should be regarded as a collective history of an interior land mass known as the Eurasian "steppe" surrounded by distinct peripheral regions including what is known today as East Asia, South Asia, and the Middle East. Some of the world's earliest known civilizations were established in Asia, particularly around the coastal regions, due to river valleys that produced rich and fertile soil thereby promoting agriculture. The interior steppe region of Eurasia, on the other hand, is notable for its mountainous geographies, dense forests, and frozen tundras which led to it being sparsely populated by nomadic tribes. The center steppe region and the coastal periphery region were separated by massive mountains and deserts, were challenging to navigate, and thus also fostered fewer human developments.

Given the lengthy timespan encompassing over 12,000 years, most researchers and historians generally divide Asian history into five notable periods. Although the first Neolithic period dates roughly from 9,000 - 4000 B.C., there is evidence of nomadic hunter-gatherers in Turkey as early as 10,000 B.C., which suggests that there are further historical artifacts that remain to be discovered. The Neolothic culture is notable, for it presents the earliest evidence of forms agricultural developments, primarily farming and rice production.

Although the second Bronze Age period generally encompasses the period from 4500 – 500 B.C., it is generally thought that the Chalcolithic period (4500 – 3500 B.C.) replaced the Neolithic culture. As the name implies, the Bronze Age is notable for its centers of metalworking, particularly in China and Vietnam, as well as the emergence of bronze artifacts, such as tools, drums, etc., in regions such as Burma, Vietnam, Thailand and Southern China.

The subsequent Iron Age (500 B.C. – 600 A.D.) represents to many the age of dynasties and empires, including the Mauryan dynasty in India, the Archaemenid dynasty of the Persian Empire in Turkey and Greece, and the Qin Dynasty in China. The following medieval Middle Ages period (600 – 1500 A.D.) is known for its development of warfare, communication and science. It also is characterized by its painting, ceramics, and architectural masterpieces.

Religion, too, developed over the centuries. Whereas Islam took over the Middle East, Caucasus and Central Asia during the Muslim conquests of the 7th century (later developing in the Indian subcontinent), the Far East was dominated by philosophies such as Buddhism, Taoism and Confucianism. The medieval period was perhaps most notable for its domination by the ruthless Khans, where Genghis Khan, his grandson Kublai Khan and the Mongol armies controlled land in China, Central Asia, the Middle East, Russia and Eastern Europe. Their empire spread as far West as Jerusalem before their defeat in the last 13th century. The medieval culture is best known for its painting, ceramics and architectural masterpieces.

The final Modern Period (1500 A.D. – present) is known for the dominance of the Russian Empire (taking control of Central Asia and Siberia), the Ottoman Empire (the Middle East and Turkey) and the Qing Dynasty (China). The European powers were also an important influence on the region during this period, as they began to control areas such as British India, French Indochina and Portuguese Goa and Macau.
Due to the long and often tumultuous history, the culture of Asia is understandably diverse. Indeed, although Asia represents to many a single "continent," it is more commonly divided into cultural subregions such as Central, East, South, North, West and Southeast Asia. Because Asia is not a distinct continent separated by oceans, there remains a diverse and non-uniform culture across the region.

East Asia is generally considered to represent China, and its enormous historical influence on proximate geographies such as Japan, Taiwan, Hong Kong, Korea and Macau. The region's languages are all based historically on shared Chinese-derived language characteristics. The Chinese script represents a unifying communication form, and as such, shares much in common with written languages in Taiwan, South Korea, Vietnam and Japan. The geographies also have commonality in religion, with a strong basis in Buddhism and Taoism, as well as a shared philosophy derived from Confucianism. Apart from these unifying influences, the countries of the region continue to exhibit much diversity in areas such as the arts, spoke languages, cuisines, music and other local traditions.

South Asia, also referred to as the "Indian subcontinent," includes the four south Indian states, as well as Bangladesh, West Bengal, Pakistan, Nepal, Bhutan, Sikkim, Sri Lanka, Arunaachal Pradesh, Jammu and Kashmir, and several smaller border states. Many of these regions share a common Dravidian language, although West Bengal and Bangladesh share Bengali languages. Indo-Aryan languages are spoken in Pakistan, Sri Lanka and Nepal. Religion in South Asia is quite varied as well. India's four major religions include Hinduism, Buddhism, Jainism and Sikhism, with other major religions represented in the region such as Christianity and Islam (predominant in Bangladesh, Pakistan).
Southeast Asia also has been greatly influenced by India and China, although the religions of Islam and Christianity have also been imported from Southwest Asia. The region includes countries such as Vietnam, Cambodia, Myanmar, Thailand, Laos, Malaysia, Singapore, East Timor, Brunei, Indonesia and the Philippines. The region continues to exhibit much Western influence, particularly countries such as the Philippines due to efforts at colonialism from the U.S. and Spain. Notable Southeast Asian cultural contributions include rice paddy agriculture, stilt houses and dance movements.
West Asia is commonly referred to as the Middle East, although the term is somewhat misleading--it is indeed east of Europe, but it is also west of India and south of Russia. The West Asia region consists of Iran, Iraq, Turkey, Syria, Armenia, Georgia, Azerbaijan, Lebanon, Jordan, Israel, Palestine (the territories), Saudi Arabia, Bahrain, Kuwait, UAE, Qatar, Oman and Yemen. Despite recent wars, Iraq is an excellent representative of the region as it has the cultural trifecta of TAP (Turkish, Arab and Persian) influence. While most would associate the region with a desert climate, the Anatolian (Turkey, Georgia, Armenia) and Persian (Iran, Azerbaijan, Afghanistan, Iraq) Plateaus present diverse terrains and more temperate climates. Among other things, the region's culture is known for its wealth of literature and diverse cuisine, the latter incorporating elements of TAP fused with Northern Africa influences.

The Central and North Asian regions have a decidedly Russian influence. The central region consists predominantly of countries that were previously part of Soviet Union, specifically Uzbekistan, Turkmenistan, Kyrgyzstan, Kazakhstan and Tajikstan. The region is predominantly Muslim, and has a long history of conquests, including rule by Mongols, Persians, Tatars, Russians and Samatians, which has resulted in a very distinct and vibrant culture. North Asia consists primarily of Russia itself, although the geographic region of Siberia, historically the land of the Tatars, is included as it succumbed to Russian rule.
If there is a single word that one could use to describe Asia it would be "diversity." There remains an abundance of ethnic groups throughout Asia, which have adapted over the years to the wide range of geographies and climates. Asia is also a region with great linguistic diversity. With few exceptions (Korea, for example), most counties have more than one language that is natively spoken. Amazingly, in India it is estimated that there are almost 1700 "mother tongues" with over 850 language dialects in current usage.
Similarly, there is enormous diversity in cultural areas such as literature, arts, philosophy and religion, and present generations are truly fortunate to have such a wealth of historical research on these topics. Because the colonization of Asia largely ceased during the 20th century, there remains a strong drive towards nationality and independence across the region. As a result, the history and culture of Asia today plays an important role in world economics and politics, as exhibited by the influence of countries such as Russia, China, Japan and India on the global stage of economic and cultural development. In short, Asia's influence on the world cannot be overstated, and this historical book series helps preserve that legacy and culture.

T.S. Wentworth

Primer on Asia: History and Culture

History of Asia

The history of Asia can be seen as the collective history of several distinct peripheral coastal regions such as, East Asia, South Asia, and the Middle East linked by the interior mass of the Eurasian steppe. The coastal periphery was the home to some of the world's earliest known civilizations, with each of the three regions developing early civilizations around fertile river valleys. These valleys were fertile because the soil there was rich and could bare many root crops. The civilizations in Mesopotamia, the Indus Valley, and China shared many similarities and likely exchanged technologies and ideas such as mathematics and the wheel. Other notions such as that of writing likely developed individually in each area. Cities, states and then empires developed in these lowlands.

The steppe region had long been inhabited by mounted nomads, and from the central steppes they could reach all areas of the Asian continent. The northern part of the continent, covering much of Siberia was also inaccessible to the steppe nomads due to the dense forests and the tundra. These areas in Siberia were very sparsely populated.

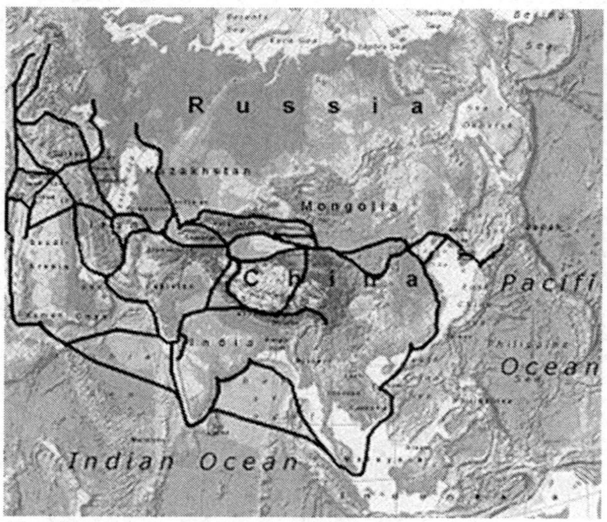

The Silk Road connected many civilisations across Asia

The center and periphery were kept separate by mountains and deserts. The Caucasus, Himalaya, Karakum Desert, and Gobi Desert formed barriers that the steppe horsemen could only cross with difficulty. While technologically and culturally the city dwellers were more advanced, they could do little militarily to defend against the mounted hordes of the steppe. However, the lowlands did not have enough open grasslands to support a large horsebound force. Thus the nomads who conquered states in China, India, and the Middle East were soon forced to adapt to the local societies.

A temple area in southeastern Turkey at Göbekli Tepe dated to 10,000 BC has been seen as the beginning of the "Neolithic 1" culture. This site was developed by nomadic hunter-gatherers since there is no permanent housing in the vicinity. This temple site is the oldest known man-made place of worship. By 8500–8000 BC farming communities began to spread to Anatolia, North Africa and north Mesopotamia.

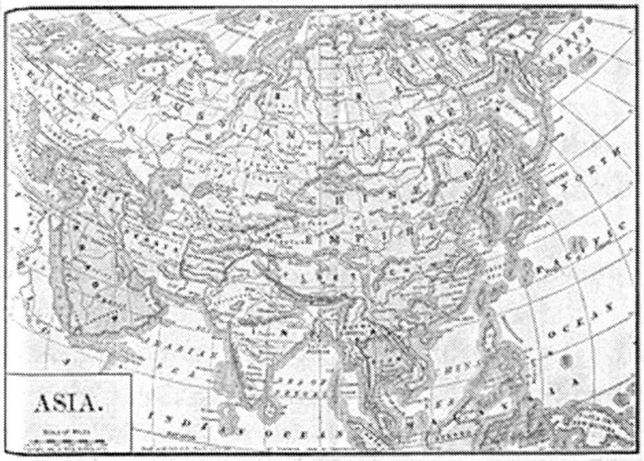

Map of Asia, 1892

A report by archaeologist Rakesh Tewari on Lahuradewa, India shows new C14 datings that range between 8000 BC and 9000 BC associated with rice, making Lahuradewa the earliest Neolithic site in entire South Asia.

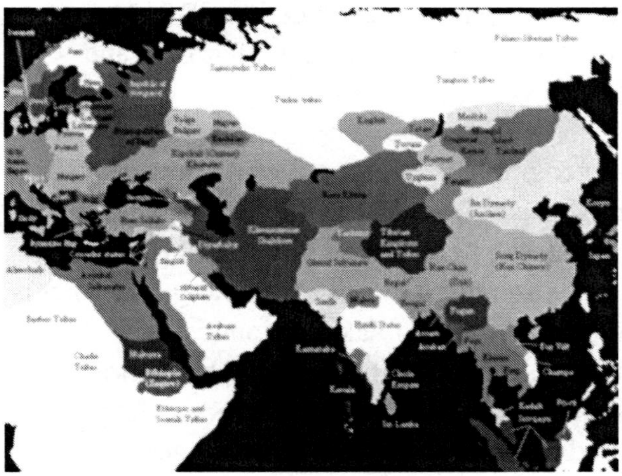

Asia in 1200 CE, just before the Mongol Empire

The prehistoric Beifudi site near Yixian in Hebei Province, China, contains relics of a culture contemporaneous with the Cishan and Xinglongwa cultures of about 7000–8000 BC, Neolithic cultures east of the Taihang Mountains, filling in an archaeological gap between the two Northern Chinese cultures. The total excavated area is more than 1,200 square meters and the collection of Neolithic findings at the site consists of two phases.

Around 5500 BCE the Halafian culture appeared in the Levant, Lebanon, Palestine, Syria, Anatolia and northern Mesopotamia, based upon dryland agriculture.

In southern Mesopotamia were the alluvial plains of Sumer and Elam. Since there was little rainfall irrigation systems were necessary. The Ubaid culture from flourished from 5500 BCE.

The Chalcolithic period began about 4500 BCE, then the Bronze Age began about 3500 BCE, replacing the Neolithic cultures. The Indus Valley Civilization (IVC) was a Bronze Age civilization (3300–1300 BCE; mature period 2600–1900 BCE) which was centered mostly in the western part of the Indian Subcontinent, considered as early form of Hinduism performed during this civilization.

China and Vietnam were also centers of metalworking. Dating back to the Neolithic Age, the first bronze drums, called the Dong Son drums have been uncovered in and around the Red River Delta regions of Vietnam and Southern China. These relate to the prehistoric Dong Son Culture of Vietnam. In Ban Chiang, Thailand (Southeast Asia), bronze artifacts have been discovered dating to 2100 BC. In Nyaunggan, Burma bronze tools have been excavated along with ceramics and stone artifacts. Dating is still currently broad (3500–500 BC).

The Achaemenid dynasty of the Persian Empire, founded by Cyrus the Great, ruled an area from Greece and Turkey to the Indus River and Central Asia during the 6th to 4th centuries BC. Alexander the Great conquered this empire in the 4th century BC. The Roman Empire would later control parts of Western Asia. The Seleucid, Parthian and Sassanian dynasties of Persia dominated Western Asia for centuries.

Foundation of the Maurya Empire which was geographically extensive and powerful empire in ancient India, ruled by the Mauryan dynasty from 321 to 185 BC. It was one of the world's largest empires in its time. At its greatest extent, the empire stretched to the north along the natural boundaries of the Himalayas, and to the east stretching into what is now Assam. To the west, it probably reached beyond modern Pakistan, annexing Balochistan and much of what is now Afghanistan, including the modern Herat and Kandahar provinces. The Gupta Empire was an Ancient Indian empire which existed approximately from 320 to 550 CE and covered much of the Indian Subcontinent. Founded by Maharaja Sri-Gupta, the dynasty was the model of a classical civilization. Maurya and Gupta empires are called as the Golden Age of India and were marked by extensive inventions and discoveries in science, technology, art, religion and philosophy that crystallized the elements of what is generally known as Indian culture. The religions of Hinduism and Buddhism, which began in India, were an important influence on South, East and Southeast Asia.

The Qin Dynasty was the first ruling dynasty of Imperial China, lasting from 221 to 206 BC. The Han Dynasty (206 BCE – 220 CE) was the second imperial dynasty of China, preceded by the Qin Dynasty and succeeded by the Three Kingdoms (220–265 CE). Spanning over four centuries, the period of the Han Dynasty is considered a golden age in Chinese history. To this day, China's majority ethnic group refers to itself as the "Han people."

Many ancient civilizations were influenced by the Silk Road, which connected China, India, the Middle East and Europe.

The Islamic Caliphate and other Islamic states took over the Middle East, Caucasus and Central Asia during the Muslim conquests of the 7th century, and later expanded into the Indian subcontinent and Malay archipelago. The Mongol Empire conquered a large part of Asia in the 13th century, an area extending from China to Europe. Marco Polo was not the first Westerner to travel to the Orient and return with amazing stories of this different culture, but his accounts published in the late 13th and early 14th centuries were the first to be widely read throughout Europe.

The Chola Dynasty of south India annexed most of southeast Asia during 10th-11th century. The Muslim conquest in the Indian subcontinent mainly took place from the 12th century onwards, though earlier Muslim conquests made limited inroads into the region, beginning during the period of the ascendancy of the Rajput Kingdoms in North India, although Sindh and Multan were captured in 8th century.

Medieval Asia had far surpassed the West in the development of warfare, communication and science. Gunpowder was widely used as early as the 11th century and they were using moveable type printing five hundred years before Gutenberg created his press. Buddhism, Taoism, Confucianism were the dominant philosophies of the Far East during the Middle Ages.

Medieval Asia was the kingdom of the Khans. Never before had any person controlled as much land as Genghis Khan. He built his power unifying separate Mongol tribes before expanding his kingdom south and west. He and his grandson, Kublai Khan, controlled lands in China, Burma, Central Asia, Russia, Iran, the Middle East, and Eastern Europe. Estimates are that the Mongol armies reduced the population of China by nearly a third. Genghis Khan was a pagan who tolerated nearly every religion except Islam, and their culture often suffered the harshest treatment from Mongol armies. The Khan armies pushed as far west as Jerusalem before being defeated in 1260.

The Middle Ages were an unsurpassed era for Chinese ceramics and painting. Medieval architectural masterpieces such as Angkor Wat in Cambodia, the Great South Gate in Todaiji, Japan, and the Tien-ning Temple in Peking, China are some of the surviving constructs from this era.

The Black Death, which would later ravage Western Europe had its beginnings in Asia, where it wiped out large populations in China in 1331. China flourished again late in the medieval era during the famed Ming Dynasty. In Japan these later Middle Age centuries saw a return to the traditional Shinto faith and the continuing popularity of Zen Buddhism.

A view of the Fort St George in 18th Century Madras.

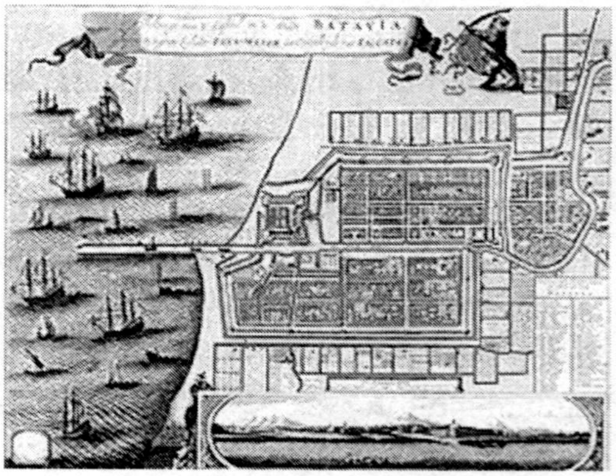

Dutch Batavia in the 17th century, built in what is now North Jakarta

The Russian Empire began to expand into Asia from the 17th century, eventually taking control of all of Siberia and most of Central Asia by the end of the 19th century. The Ottoman Empire controlled Turkey and the Middle East from the 16th century onwards. In the 17th century, the Manchu conquered China and established the Qing Dynasty, although this was in decline by the nineteenth century and had been overthrown in 1912.

The European powers had control of other parts of Asia by the 1900s, such as British India, French Indochina and Portuguese Macau and Goa. The Great Game between Russia and Britain was the struggle for power in the Central Asian region in the nineteenth century. The Trans-Siberian Railway, crossing Asia by train, was complete by 1916. Parts of Asia remained free from European control, although not influence, such as Persia, Thailand and most of China. In the twentieth century, Imperial Japan expanded into China and Southeast Asia during the Second World War. After the war, many Asian countries became independent from European powers. During the Cold War, the northern parts of Asia were communist controlled with the Soviet Union and People's Republic of China, while western allies formed pacts such as CENTO and SEATO. Conflicts such as the Korean War, Vietnam War and Soviet invasion of Afghanistan were fought between communists and anti-communists. In the decades after the Second World War, a massive restructuring plan drove Japan to become the world's second-largest economy, a phenomenon known as the Japanese post-war economic miracle. The Arab-Israeli conflict has dominated much of the recent history of the Middle East. After the Soviet Union's collapse in 1991, there were many new independent nations in Central Asia.

Today China, India, Japan, and Russia play important role in world economics and politics.

Culture of Asia

The continent of Asia is commonly divided into more natural geographic and cultural subregions, including the Central Asia, East Asia, South Asia (the "Indian subcontinent"), North Asia, West Asia and Southeast Asia. Geographically, Asia is not a distinct continent; culturally, there has been little unity or common history for many of the cultures and peoples of Asia.

Asian art, music, and cuisine, as well as literature, are important parts of Asian culture. Eastern philosophy and religion also plays a major role, with Hinduism, Taoism, Confucianism, Buddhism, Christianity and Islam; all playing major roles. One of the most complex parts of Asian culture is the relationship between traditional cultures and the Western world.

There are an abundance of ethnic groups throughout Asia, each having adapted to their local climate and landscape. On the coasts of Asia, ethnic groups have adopted various methods of harvesting and transport. Some groups are primarily hunter-gatherers, some practice a nomadic lifestyle, others have been agrarian/rural for millennia, while others are becoming industrial/urban. Some groups/countries of Asia are completely urban

(Singapore and Hong Kong). The colonization of Asia was largely ended in the twentieth century by national drives for independence and self-determination across the continent.

East Asia

East Asia is usually thought to consist of China, Japan, Korea, Hong Kong, Macau and Taiwan. The dominant influence historically has been China, though in modern times, cultural exchange has flowed more bidirectionally. Major characteristics of this region include shared Chinese-derived language characteristics, as well as shared religion, especially Buddhism and Taoism. There is also a shared social and moral philosophy derived from Confucianism.

The Chinese script is the oldest continuously used writing system in the world, and has long been a unifying principle of East Asia, as the medium for conveying Chinese culture. It was historically used throughout the region, and is still used in by ethnic Chinese throughout the world, as well as in Japan and to a lesser extent South Korea. Within China, the meanings of the characters remain generally unchanged from region to region, though their pronunciations differ. This is because Classical Chinese was long the written language of all China, and was replaced by Mandarin as the national written language in the twentieth century. For example, a Cantonese and a Mandarin speaker cannot hold a conversation, but if they are educated they can understand each other in writing, as they both learned to read and write Mandarin in school. To a lesser extent, Taiwanese, South Koreans, and Japanese can all understand something of the Chinese characters that the other writes, though this is no longer the case with China, due to simplifications of the characters there.

Chinese writing was passed on to Korea, Japan and Vietnam. In Japan, where it (called Kanji in Japan) now forms a major component of the Japanese writing system. In the 9th century, Japanese developed their own writing systems called Kana (Hiragana and Katakana) which support Kanji script to suit Japanese language. Today, both ideograph Kanji and syllabary Kana is used in mixture in Japanese. In Vietnam, Chinese script (Han Tu) was used during the millennium under the influence of China, with the vernacular Chu Nom script are also used since 13th century. However, this has now (since the early 20th century) been replaced completely by the Latin Alphabet-based Quoc Ngu. In the 15th century, Koreans also developed their own writing system called Han-gul which is more adapted script to write Korean.

In these cultures, especially in China and Japan the educational level of person is traditionally measured by the quality of his or her calligraphy, rather than diction, as is sometimes the case in the West.

Though Korea and Japan are not Chinese speaking regions, their languages have been influenced by Chinese to some extent. Even though their writing systems have changed over time, Chinese is still found in the historical roots of many borrowed words. Though in modern times, Chinese is also influenced by other Asian languages, especially modern technical and political terms created in Japan to represent western concepts. For example, 文化 (culture), 文明 (civilization), 人民 (people), 経済 (economy), 共和 (republic) and 哲学 (philosophy) are borrowed words from Japanese to Chinese. (ja: 和製漢語, zh: 和製漢語)

Apart from the unifying influence of Confucianism, Buddhism, Chinese characters, and other Chinese Cultural Influences, there is nevertheless much diversity between the countries of the region such as different religions, national costumes, languages, writing systems, cuisines, traditional musics and so on.

South Asia (Indian Subcontinent)

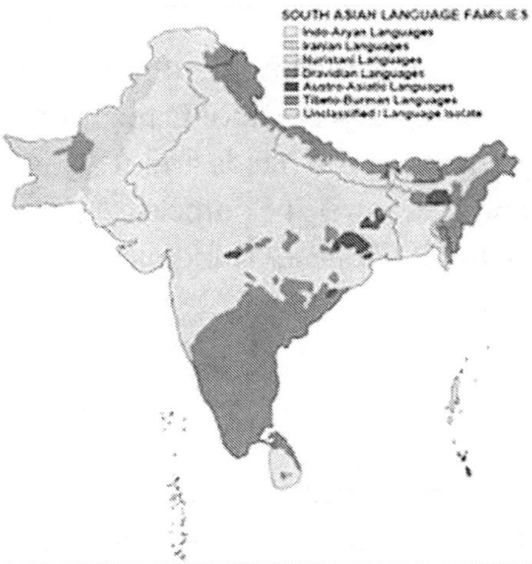

Language families in South Asia

The four South Indian states and Sri Lanka share a Dravidian culture, due to the prominence of Dravidian languages there. Bangladesh and the state of West Bengal share a common heritage and culture based on the Bengali language.

Nepal, Bhutan, the states of Sikkim, Arunachal Pradesh, Ladakh in the state of Jammu and Kashmir and parts of the states of Himachal Pradesh, Uttaranchal have a great cultural similarity to Tibet, Tibetan Buddhism being the dominant religion there. Finally the border states of Assam, Meghalaya, Mizoram, Manipur, Nagaland and Tripura have cultural affinities with South East Asia.

Hinduism, Buddhism, Jainism and Sikhism, the four major world religions founded in the region that is today's India, are spread throughout the subcontinent. Islam and Christianity also have significant region-specific histories. While 80% of Indians are Hindus and

Nepal is a Hindu-majority State, Sri Lanka and Bhutan have a majority of Buddhists. Islam is the predominant religion of Bangladesh, Pakistan.

Traditional Rajasthani garments from Jaipur,

Indo-Aryan languages are spoken in Pakistan, Sinhalese of Sri Lanka and most of North, West, and East India and Nepal. Dravidian languages are spoken in South India and in Sri Lanka by Tamil community. Tibeto-Burman languages are spoken in the North and North East India.

Southeast Asia

Southeast Asia consists of Vietnam and Maritime Southeast Asia. Southeast Asia is usually thought to include Myanmar, the Philippines, Thailand, Laos, Cambodia, Mainland Southeast Asia, Malaysia, Singapore, East Timor, Brunei and Indonesia. The region has been greatly influenced by the cultures and religions of India and China as well as the religions Islam and Christianity from Southwest Asia. Southeast Asia has also had much Western influence due to the lasting legacy of colonialism. One example is the Philippines which has been heavily influenced by America and Spain due to the invasion.

A common feature found around the region are stilt houses. Another shared feature is rice paddy agriculture, which originated in Southeast Asia thousands of years ago. Dance is also a very important feature of the culture, utilizing movements of the hands and feet perfected over thousands of years. Furthermore, the arts and literature of Southeast Asia is very distinctive as some have been influenced by Indian, Hindu, Chinese, Buddhist and Islamic literature.

West Asia

West Asia largely corresponds with the term the Middle East. However, the usage of the term Middle East is slowly fading out due to its obvious Eurocentrism as the region is east of Europe but it is south of Russia and west of India. West Asia consists of Turkey, Syria, Armenia, Georgia, Azerbaijan, Iraq, Iran, Lebanon, Jordan, Israel, Palestinian territories, Saudi Arabia, Kuwait, Bahrain, Qatar, United Arab Emirates, Oman and Yemen. The region is the historical birthplace of Abrahamic religions: Judaism, Christianity and Islam. Today, the region is almost 93% Muslim and is dominated by Islamic politics. Culturally, the region is Turkish, Arab and Persian. Iraq is a unique example of both Persian, Turkish and Arab culture. Many of the Arab countries are desert and thus many nomadic groups exist today. On the other hand, modern metropolises also exist on the shifting sands: Abu Dhabi, Amman, Riyadh, Doha and Muscat. The climate is mostly of a desert climate however some of the coastal regions have a more temperate climate. On the other hand, the Anatolian plateau (Turkey, Georgia, Armenia) is very mountainous and thus has a more temperate climate while the coasts have a distinct Mediterranean climate. The Persian Plateau (Iran, Azerbaijan, Afghanistan, Iraq and Turkmenistan) has a diverse terrain, it is mainly mountainous with portions of desert, steppe and tropical forest on the coast of the Caspian Sea. West Asian cuisine is a fusion of Turkish, Arabian, North African and Persian cuisine. It is immensely rich and diverse. The literature is also immensely rich with Arabic, Turkish and Persian literature dominating. One of the most famous literary works of West Asia is 1001 Arabian Nights.

Central Asia

Central Asia is deemed to consist of the five former Soviet Socialist Republics: Kazakhstan, Kyrgyzstan, Tajikstan, Uzbekistan and Turkmenistan. However, Iran, Afghanistan and Pakistan are sometimes included. The predominant religion in Central Asia is Islam. Central Asia has a long rich history mainly based on its historic position on the famous Silk Road. It has been conquered by Mongols, Persians, Tatars, Russians, Sarmatian and thus has a very distinct, vibrant culture. The culture is influenced by Chinese, Indian, Persian, Arabian, Turkish, Russian, Sarmatian and Mongolian cultures. The people of the steppes of Central Asia have historically been nomadic people but a unifying state was established in Central Asia in the 16th century: The Kazakh Khanate. The music of Central Asia is rich and varied and is appreciated worldwide. Meanwhile, Central Asian cuisine is one of the most prominent cuisines of Asia, with cuisines from Pakistan, India, China and Azerbaijan showing significant influence from the foods of Central Asia. One of the most famous Central Asian foods are manti and pilaf.
The literature of Central Asia is linked with Persian literature as historically it has been part of the Persian Empire for a lot of its history. Furthermore, being at the junction of the Silk Road it has numerous Chinese, Indian and Arabian literary works.

North Asia

For the most part, North Asia is considered to be made up of the Asian part of Russia solely. The geographic region of Siberia was the historical land of the Tatars in the Siberia Khanate. However Russian expansion essentially undermined this and thus today it is under Russian rule. There are roughly 40 million people living in North Asia.

Architecture

A typical example of Dravidian Architecture

In Japan, some wooden temples of Nara are over 1,000 years old. Although some parts have been replaced, much of the original structure is said to be intact. Ise Shrine, also a wooden structure, is completely rebuilt in exactly the same style every 20 years. The primary reason behind this may relate to the ancient Japanese imitation of rebirth in nature and the impermanence of all things. This practice also helps to preserve traditional carpentry skills and techniques (building without nails). Wooden castles were destroyed or dismantled during the shift from feudalism in the Meiji Restoration. Intact examples are Himeji Castle (17th century) and Hikone Castle (15th century). Reconstructed examples are Osaka Castle and Himeji Castle.

Other cultures might build from stone, but the jungles and forests might overgrow the buildings, as in Angkor Wat.

Central Asian Music

The music of Central Asia is as vast and unique as the many cultures and peoples who inhabit the region. The one constant throughout the musical landscape is Islam, which defines the music's focus and the musicians' inspiration.

Principal instrument types are two- or three-stringed lutes, the necks either fretted or fretless; fiddles made of horsehair; flutes, mostly open at both ends and either end-blown or side-blown; and Jews' harps, either metal or, often in Siberia, wooden. Percussion instruments include frame drums, tambourines, and kettledrums.

Instrumental polyphony is achieved primarily by lutes and fiddles. On the other hand, vocal polyphony is achieved in different ways: Bashkirs hum a basic pitch while playing solo flute.

Gongs from Indonesia

Southeast Asian Music

In the Punjab region of India and Pakistan, bhangra dance is very popular. The bhangra is a celebration of the harvest. The people dance to the beat of a drum while singing and dancing.

In Thailand which is never colonized by Western countries, has retained cultural connections with the two of the great centers of Asian civilizations, India and China. Dances of Burma, a country which was colonized only for a brief period, also retain very strong influences from these cultures.

In Southeast Asia, dance is an integral part of the culture; the styles of dance vary from island to island. There are courtly dances, found, for example, wherever there are Rajahs and princesses. There are also dances of celebration. For example, according to oral history, in 1212, when 10 Bornean datus left the rule of Sri Vijayan empire on Borneo, they sailed away and negotiated settlement rights with the chieftain of the Negritos on the island of Panay. In commemoration of the agreement, they danced; the Negritos danced as well.

Mythology and folklore

Vishnu as Matsya.

The story of Great Floods find reference in most of the regions of Asia. The Hindu mythology tells about an avatar of God Vishnu in the form of a fish who warned Manu of a terrible flood. In ancient Chinese mythology Shan Hai Jing, the Chinese ruler Da Yu had to spend ten years to control a deluge which swept out most of the ancient China and was aided by the goddess Nuwa who literally "fixed" the "broken" sky through which huge rains were pouring.

The regions of Asia has a rich variety of mythical fauna. Japan has Nekomatas, cats with two tails and having magical powers; whereas Balinese mythology has child-eating Rangdas. Hindu mythology have Pishachas haunting the cremation grounds to eat half-burnt human corpses, and Bhuts hanting the desolate places. Asia has a rich tradition of folklores and storytelling. In the Indian subcontinent, the Panchatantra, a collection of fables 200 BC, has remained a favorite for 2000 years.

Languages

Asia is a continent with great linguistic diversity, and is home to various language families and many language isolates. A majority of Asian countries have more than one language that is natively spoken. For instance, according to Ethnologue over 600 languages are spoken in Indonesia while over 100 are spoken in the Philippines. The official figure of 'mother tongues' spoken in India is 1683, of which an estimated 850 are in daily use. Korea, on the other hand, is home to only one language.

The main language families found in Asia, along with examples of each, are:

- Austro-Asiatic: Khasi, Khmer, Mundari, Vietnamese
- Austronesian: Atayal, Cebuano, Cham, Ilokano, Indonesian, Javanese, Malay, Paiwan, Sundanese, Tagalog, Tetum
- Dravidian: Kannada, Malayalam, Tamil, Telugu
- Indo-Asiatic: Armenian, Bengali, English, Gujarati, Marathi, Hindi, Kurdish, Nepali, Pashto, Persian, Portuguese, Punjabi, Russian, Konkani, Sanskrit, Tajik, Urdu
- Japonic: Japanese, Okinawan

- Sino-Tibetan:
- Sinitic: Mandarin, Gan, Hakka, Min, Wu, Xiang, Yue
- Tibeto-Burman: Tibetan, Burmese
- Tai-Kadai: Lao, Thai
- Turkic: Azeri, Kazakh, Kyrgyz, Tatar, Turkish, Turkmen, Uzbek
- Afro-Asiatic: Arabic, Aramaic, Canaanite, Berber, Hebrew
- Other languages that do not belong to the above groups include Ainu, Burushaski, Georgian, Hmong, Korean, Mongolian, various Romance-based creoles (Chavacano, Macanese, and Kristang) and many others.

Asian Literature

Classical Indian Literature

The famous poet and playwright Kālidāsa wrote two epics: Raghuvamsha (Dynasty of Raghu) and Kumarasambhava (Birth of Kumar Kartikeya); they were written in Classical Sanskrit rather than Epic Sanskrit. Other examples of works written in Classical Sanskrit include the Pānini's Ashtadhyayi which standardized the grammar and phonetics of Classical Sanskrit. The Laws of Manu is an important text in Hinduism. Kālidāsa is often considered to be the greatest playwright in Sanskrit literature, and one of the greatest poets in Sanskrit literature, whose Recognition of Shakuntala and Meghaduuta are the most famous Sanskrit plays. He occupies the same position in Sanskrit literature that Shakespeare occupies in English literature. Some other famous plays were Mricchakatika by Shudraka, Svapna Vasavadattam by Bhasa, and Ratnavali by Sri Harsha. Later poetic works include Geeta Govinda by Jayadeva. Some other famous works are Chanakya's Arthashastra and Vatsyayana's Kamasutra.

Classical Chinese Literature

In Tang and Song dynasty China, famous poets such as Li Bai authored works of great importance. They wrote shī (Classical Chinese: 詩) poems, which have lines with equal numbers of characters, as well as cí (詞) poems with mixed line varieties.

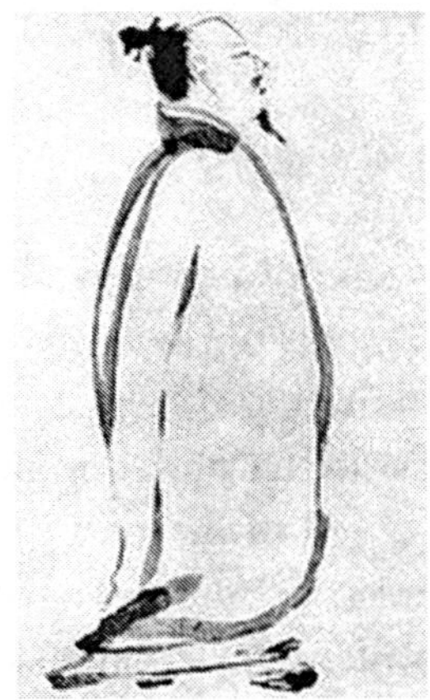

Tang dynasty Chinese poet Li Bai, in a 13th century depiction by Liang Kai.

Classical Japanese Literature

In the early eleventh century, court lady Murasaki Shikibu wrote Tale of the Genji considered the masterpiece of Japanese literatures and an early example of a work of fiction in the form of a novel. Early-Modern Japanese literature (17th–19th centuries) developed comparable innovations such as haiku, a form of Japanese poetry that evolved from the ancient hokku (Japanese language: 発句) mode. Haiku consists of three lines: the first and third lines each have five morae (the rough phonological equivalent of syllables), while the second has seven. Original haiku masters included such figures as Edo period poet Matsuo Bashō (松尾芭蕉); others influenced by Bashō include Kobayashi Issa and Masaoka Shiki.

Nobel Laureates

Rabindranath Tagore, the first Asian Nobel laureate.

The polymath Rabindranath Tagore, a Bengali poet, dramatist, and writer from India, became in 1913 the first Asian Nobel laureate. He won his Nobel Prize in Literature for notable impact his prose works and poetic thought had on English, French, and other national literatures of Europe and the Americas. He also wrote Jana Gana Mana the national anthem of India as well as Amar Shonar Bangla the national anthem of Bangladesh. Later, other Asian writers won Nobel Prizes in literature, including Yasunari Kawabata (Japan, 1966), and Kenzaburo Oe (Japan, 1994).

Philosophy

Asian philosophical traditions originated in India and China, and has been classified as Eastern philosophy covering a large spectrum of philosophical thoughts and writings, including those popular within India and China. The Indian philosophy include Hindu and Buddhist philosophies. They include elements of nonmaterial pursuits, whereas another school of thought Cārvāka, which originated in India, and was propuned by Charvak around 2500 years before, preached the enjoyment of material world. Middle Eastern philosophy include Islamic philosophy as well as Persian philosophy.

During the 20th century, in the two most populous countries of Asia, two dramatically different political philosophies took shape. Gandhi gave a new meaning to Ahimsa, and redefined the concepts of nonviolence and nonresistance. During the same period, Mao Zedong's communist philosophy was crystallized.

Religions

A stone image of the Buddha.

Hinduism, Buddhism, Jainism and Sikhism originated in India, a country of South Asia. In East Asia, particularly in China and Japan, Confucianism, Taoism, Zen Buddhism and Shinto took shape. Other religions of Asia include the Bahá'í Faith, Shamanism practiced in Siberia, and Animism practiced in the eastern parts of the Indian subcontinent.

Today 30% of Muslims live in the South Asian region, mainly in Pakistan, India, Bangladesh and the Maldives. The world's largest single Muslim community (within the bounds of one nation) is in Indonesia. There are also significant Muslim populations in the Philippines, Brunei, Malaysia, China, Russia, Iran, Central Asia and West Asia.

In the Philippines and East Timor, Roman Catholicism is the predominant religion; it was introduced by the Spaniards and the Portuguese, respectively. In Armenia, Armenian Apostolic Church is the predominant religion. Various Christian sects have adherents in portions of the Middle East.

Judaism is the major religion of Israel.

A large majority of people in the world who practice a religious faith practice one founded in Asia. Religions founded in Asia and with a majority of their contemporary adherents in Asia include:

- Bahá'í Faith: slightly more than half of all adherents are in Asia
- Buddhism: Cambodia, China, Japan, Korea, Laos, Malaysia, Mongolia, Burma, Singapore, Sri Lanka, Thailand, Vietnam, parts of northern, eastern, and western India, and parts of central and eastern Russia (Siberia).
- Mahayana Buddhism: China, Japan, Korea, Malaysia, Singapore, Vietnam.
- Theravada Buddhism: Cambodia, parts of China, Laos, mainly northern parts of Malaysia, Burma, Sri Lanka, Thailand, as well as parts of Vietnam.

- Vajrayana Buddhism: Parts of China, Mongolia, parts of northern and eastern India, parts of central and eastern Russia and Siberia.
- Hinduism: India, Nepal, Bangladesh, Sri Lanka, Pakistan, Malaysia, Singapore, Bali.
- Islam: Central, South and Southwest Asia, Indonesia, Malaysia, Philippines, and Brunei.
- Ahmadiyya Islam: Pakistan, Bangladesh, India.
- Shia Islam: largely to specific Iran, Azerbaijan, parts of Iraq, Bahrain, parts of Afghanistan, parts of India, parts of Pakistan.
- Sunni Islam: dominant in the rest of the regions mentioned above.
- Jainism: India
- Shinto: Japan
- Sikhism: India and Malaysia
- Taoism (Daoism): China, Vietnam, Singapore, and Taiwan
- Zoroastrianism: Iran, India, Pakistan
- Shamanism: Japan (Itako), Korea, Siberia
- Animism: Eastern India
- Religions founded in Asia that have the majority of their contemporary adherents in other regions include:
- Christianity (Lebanon, Syria, Palestine, Armenia, Georgia, South Korea, Singapore, Malaysia, Indonesia, East Timor, Pakistan, India. Vietnam and the Philippines)
- Judaism (slightly fewer than half of its adherents reside in Asia; Israel, Iran, India, Syria.)

Festivals & Celebrations

Asia has a variety of festivals and celebrations. In China, Chinese New Year, Dragon Boat Festival, and Mid-Autumn Moon Festival are traditional holidays, while National Day is a holiday of the People's Republic of China.

In Japan, Japanese New Year, National Foundation Day, Children's Day, O-bon, The Emperor's Birthday, and Christmas are popular. According to Japanese syncretism, most Japanese celebrate Buddhism's O-bon in midsummer, Shinto's Shichi-Go-San in November, and Christmas and Hatsumoude in winter together.

In India, Republic Day and Independence Day are important national festivals celebrated by people irrespective of faith. Major Hindu festivals of India include Diwali, Dussehra or Daserra, Holi, Makar Sankranti, Pongal, Mahashivratri, Ugadi, Navratri, Ramanavami, Baisakhi, Onam, Rathayatra, Ganesh Chaturthi, and Krishna Janmastami. Islamic festivals such as Eid ul-Fitr and Eid ul-Adha, Sikh festivals such as Vaisakhi, and Christian festivals such as Christmas, are also celebrated in India.

The Philippines is also tagged as the "Fiesta Country" because of its all-year-round celebrations nationwide. There is a very strong Spanish influence in their festivals, thus making the Philippines, distinctively occidental. Fiesta is the term used to refer to a festival. Most of these fiestas are celebrated in honor of a patron Saint. To summarize it all, at least every municipality has a fiesta. Some prime examples include Sinulog from Cebu and Iloilo's Dinagyang.

Food & Drinks

Chicken tikka, a well-known dish across the globe, reflects the amalgamation of Indian cooking styles with those from Central Asia.

In many parts of Asia, rice is a staple food, and it is mostly served steamed or as a porridge known as congee. China is the world largest producer and consumer of rice. In China, Japan, Korea and Vietnam, people usually use chopsticks to eat traditional food, but shapes of chopsticks are different in these countries. For example, Japanese chopsticks are spire to eat bony fish easily. Korean chopsticks are made of metal. It is said that wood is rarer than metal in Korean peninsular and metal chopsticks can prevent to poison. An island nation surrounded by ocean, Japan has various fish dishes. Especially, fresh raw fish cuisines are very popular in Japan and well-known as Sushi and Sashimi.

In India, people often eat food with their hands, and many spices are used in every dish. Most spices originated around India or neighboring countries such as Sri Lanka. Durians are a common fruit in Southeast Asia, which, Alfred Russel Wallace, attested to its delicious flavor as worth the entire cost of his trip there. In every special Filipino banquet, people will see a unique set of dishes compared to other Asian cuisine. Because of the country's long years of colonization and interactions with other neighboring cultures and nations, it has inherited Latin, Malay, Chinese, and American influences to its people's local blend.

Tamil Cuisine is popular in South India, Sril Lanka and South-East Asia.

Source: Wikipedia

A GUIDE

TO THE

OLD PERSIAN INSCRIPTIONS

BY

HERBERT CUSHING TOLMAN, Ph. D. (YALE)

FOREIGN MEMBER OF THE ROYAL ASIATIC SOCIETY OF GREAT BRITAIN AND IRELAND; ASSISTANT PROFESSOR OF SANSKRIT IN THE UNIVERSITY OF WISCONSIN

NEW YORK ∴ CINCINNATI ∴ CHICAGO ∴ BOSTON ∴ ATLANTA
AMERICAN BOOK COMPANY

TO

MY HONORED TEACHER,

WILLIAM DWIGHT WHITNEY, Ph. D., LL. D.

under whose instruction and guidance were spent five years of my study in the Sanskrit language,

this volume is

RESPECTFULLY DEDICATED.

TO THE READER.

This book does not claim to be a contribution to Iranian subjects. In these recent years there has been such an advancement in this line of scholarship that Sanskrit students have been compelled to surrender this field to specialists among whom in America the name of Dr A. V Williams Jackson of Columbia College is conspicuous In 1862 Haug published an outline of Avesta grammar in the first edition of his essays. At that time seventy octavo pages were sufficient to contain the discovered material Two years later Justi's grammar of one hundred and fifteen octavo pages was looked upon as practically exhaustive. The grammar of Spiegel appeared in 1867, that of de Harlez in 1878, that of Geiger in 1879 Kavasji Edalji's grammar (1891) and Jackson's grammar (1892) extend four fold the horizon of Avestan scholarship as contrasted with the outline presented by Haug thirty years before, although the same quantity of text of the Avesta is the basis for grammatical work. This statement can enable the reader to realize the great strides this study has made during a few years My work in the Zend Avesta and in the dialects of Persia has been simply an avocation from my chosen field of Sanskrit.

No book has been published in English containing the grammar, text and vocabulary of all the Old Persian Inscriptions It was this fact that induced the author in 1891 to issue a little volume entitled "Old Persian Grammar" the copies of which have now been sold. The first fifty pages of the present volume, which contain the grammatical principles, are based on this work

The following features characterize this volume on Old Persian Inscriptions

(1.) The grammatical principles arranged as a grammar of the language

(2.) The complete classification of all the verb-forms occurring in the inscriptions.

(3.) The transliterated text The portion supplied by conjecture has been inserted without brackets unless the conjectural reading be doubtful

(4.) The references at the bottom of the page in the text which call the attention of the student to the grammar on the first occurrence of a form or principle.

(5.) The cuneiform text.

(6.) The translation.

(7.) The vocabulary giving the related words in Sanskrit, Latin, Gothic, Anglo-Saxon, etc.

The author recommends to the reader the following books as being of interest in the history of the early decipherment of the inscriptions:

(1.) Die altpersischen Keilinschriften nach Hrn. Westergaards Mittheilungen. Zeitschrift für die Kunde des Morgenlandes herausgegeben von Dr. Christian Lassen. Leipzig, 1845.

(2.) Die persischen Keilinschriften mit Uebersetzung und Glossar von Theodor Benfey. Leipzig, 1847.

(3.) The Journal of the Royal Asiatic Society of Great Britain and Ireland, Vol. X, by H. C. Rawlinson. London, 1847.

(4.) Mémoire sur les inscriptions des Achéménides, conçues dans l' idiome des anciens Persans, par M. Oppert. Journal Asiatique ou recueil de mémoires d' extraits et de notices relatifs à l' histoire, à la philosophie, aux langues et à la litterature des peuples orientaux. Paris, 1851, 1852.

(5.) Expédition scientifique en Mésopotamie exécutée par ordre du Gouvernement de 1851 à 1854 par MM. Fulgence Fresnel, Félix Thomas et Jules Oppert, T. II. pp. 154–256.

(6.) Memoir on the Scythic Version of the Behistan Inscription by Edwin Norris, M. R. A. S. (Journal of the Royal Asiatic Society, Vol. XV. 1855.)

(7.) Mémoire sur les rapports de l' Égypte et de l' Assyrie dans l' antiquité éclaircis par l' étude des textes cunéiformes, par M. Jules Oppert. Paris, 1869.

(8.) Die altpersischen Keilinschriften im Grundtexte mit Uebersetzung. Fr. Spiegel, Leipzig, (two editions).

(9.) Zur Erklärung der altpersischen Keilinschriften von Dr. H. Kern. Zeitschrift der Deutschen morgenländischen Gesellschaft, Band XXIII, 1869.

(10.) Inscriptiones Palæo-Persicae. Cajetan Kossowicz, St. Petersburg. 1872.

In my references to foreign journals, I have used abbreviations as little as possible They are mostly of the nature of the following and need not be explained.

ZDMG = *Zeitschrift der Deutschen morgenländischen Gesellshaft*; *f vergl. Sprachforsch.* = *für vergleichende Sprachforschung*; *idg.* = *indogermanische*; *ai* = *altindische*; *Wb* = *Wörterbuch*, etc , etc.

The author is aware of the many faults this book contains as fully as the severest critic can be, and he shall be glad to receive all suggestions which may make it more useful to the reader.

HERBERT CUSHING TOLMAN.

Madison, Wisconsin, November 4th, 1892.

TABLE OF CONTENTS.

ABBREVIATIONS.

AOR.,	Aorist
A. S.,	Anglo Saxon
AVEST.,	Avestan
CF.,	Compare
ENG.,	English
GERM.,	German
GOTH.,	Gothic
IMPF.,	Imperfect
IMPV.,	Imperative
INF.,	Infinitive
LAT.,	Latin
PART.,	Participle
PERF.	Perfect
PRES.,	Present
SKT.,	Sanskrit
SLAV.,	Slavonic
1. S., etc.,	1st person singular, etc.
1. P., etc.,	1st person plural, etc.

PREFACE.

The Old Persian language deserves a larger place in American scholarship than it has yet received. Heretofore the work has been left entirely to European scholars, and it is due to a desire to awaken an interest in this old tongue among scholars of our own country that this little book has come into existence. I take the opportunity of expressing my gratitude to my pupil, WOLCOTT WEBSTER ELLSWORTH, a graduate of Yale and a member of the American Oriental Society, for help furnished me. He has taken my manuscript, which was in most part in the form of lectures, and arranged the whole work for the press. He also rendered much service in the transliteration of the cuneiform text.

I shall gladly receive all suggestions or corrections which may make this volume more helpful in imparting enthusiasm in the study of this our sister tongue.

H. C. T.

New Haven, Conn., June, 1891.

PREFACE TO SECOND EDITION.

The copies of the first edition are exhausted. The author has taken this opportunity to revise and amplify the whole work. He wishes to express his gratification for the kind reception the previous edition has received and also to make acknowledgment of many valuable suggestions.

H. C. T.

Madison, Wis., Aug., 1892.

INTRODUCTION.

Professor Grotefend was the pioneer in the decipherment of the cuneiform text. His first discovery was announced in the Literary Gazette of Göttingen, in the year 1802. About one-third of the Old Persian alphabet was determined by his transliteration of the names of Cyrus, Darius, Xerxes and Hystaspes. Professor Rask added to this number the two characters representing M and N. A memoir of M. Burnouf published in June, 1836, and a work of Professor Lassen published at Bonn in May, 1836, entitled Die Alt-Persischen Keil-Inschriften von Persepolis, furnished a true determination of twelve additional characters. Dr. Beer, of Leipzig, in a review published in Allgemein. Hall. Literat. Zeitung in the year 1838, announced the discovery of the two characters for H and Y. M. Jacquet is said to have made the same discoveries independently at Paris, and also identified the equivalents for C and JH.

It is evident that a cursive style of writing was employed for epistolary purposes and had an existence contemporaneous with the cuneiform, since the character of the latter rendered it fit only for lapidary uses, [Cf. Daniel VI, 9; Nehemiah II, 9; Herodotus VII, 100.]. No Persian cuneiform writing appears after the time of Artaxerxes Ochus, and we are safe in saying that it died out at the end of the rule of the Achæmenian kings.

The oldest inscription is that of Cyrus the Great, which perhaps may be his sepulchral inscription although the epitaph quoted by Strabo and Ctesias differs from the one on this Old Persian monument. The latest is the inscription of Artaxerxes Ochus which exhibits many peculiarities of grammatical structure indicating the decay of the language. In this inscription two compound characters for BUM and DAH are introduced (cf. Cuneiform alphabet); also before this time in the tablets of Xerxes appears an ideogram for KHSHAY*A*THIY*A*, due undoubtedly to Semitic influences.

The most important of the inscriptions is the great inscription of Darius carved upon the sacred mountain Behistan [B*A*G*A* and ST*A*N*A* *place of God*]. This immense rock rose to a perpendicular height of 1700 feet from the plain below. On this conspicuous place Darius Hystaspes caused to be inscribed the history of his reign to be a legacy to succeeding generations. The figures of Darius and his attendants are executed with considerable skill, yet inferior to that shown in the bas-reliefs of Persepolis. Before Darius stand nine usurpers to the throne bound with a cord about their necks, while under the foot of the king lies the prostrate form of another. These are intentionally of rude design and small stature. Above the picture is the effigy of the Persian god Auramazda.

The Old Persian language is most closely related to the Vedic dialect of the Sanskrit, yet the interpretation of the inscriptions depends upon the combined aid of the Sanskrit and Avestan together with the surviving dialects of Persia which have been in any degree faithful to their mother tongue. Where the cognate or derivative word fails to appear in them, an arbitrary meaning must be assigned to the Old Persian to suit the context; hence I have given in the vocabulary the authority of the related languages for the signification of each word, wherever such authority can be obtained.

GRAMMAR.

PART I.

EUPHONY.

1. A conventional arrangement of the European letters, transliterating the Old Persian cuneiform characters, is as follows:

Vowels, simple { guttural, *a*, a. / palatal, i. / labial, u.

Diphthongs { palatal, *a*i, ai. / labial, *a*u, au.

Mutes,		SURD.	SURD. ASP.	SONANT.	NASAL.
	guttural,	k	kh	g	—
	palatal,	c	—	j	—
	dental,	t	th	d	n
	labial,	p	f	b	m

Semivowels { palatal, y. / lingual, r. / labial, v.

Sibilants { lingual, sh. / dental, s.

Aspiration, h.

NOTE 1. The short a has no written sign (in the cuneiform text) unless it be initial. Therefore *a* (italic) has been used for this vowel in the transliteration. But when it is initial the same sign is employed for short a as for long a (vide infra), since the native characters make no distinction; e. g., ad*a*m

NOTE 2. The long a is transliterated in all cases by a simple a (in Roman type), e. g., Pars*a*.

EUPHONIC COMBINATION.

2. Two similar vowels coalesce, forming the corresponding long vowel; thus, p*a*sav*a* for p*a*sa and av*a*.

Actual examples can be cited of no vowels coalescing except a-vowels, yet undoubtedly should other successive vowels occur, they would suffer the above treatment.

3. The short *a* combines with a following i-vowel and u-vowel to *a*i and *a*u respectively; thus, Pars*a*iy for Pars*a* + iy; the long **a** to **ai** and **au**; thus, aniyauva for aniya + uva.

NOTE An example of **a** and **i** forming *a*i (as in the Sanskrit the long **a** and **i** combine into **e** [*a*i]) instead of **ai**, is found in the compound p*a*r*a*ita for p*a*ra and ita.

4. An i-vowel and u-vowel interpose their corresponding semivowel before a dissimilar vowel; thus, bumiya, bumi + a; isuvam, isu + am. Sometimes, however, the vowel is converted into its semivowel (especially if it be the final vowel of a diphthong); thus, ab*a*v*a*, for ab*a*u + a.

For exception, cf dur*a*i*a*piy

5. No vowel (except *a* and **a**) nor diphthong can end a word. There is inserted as a protection the corresponding semivowel; thus, up*a*riy, for up*a*ri; patuv, for patu; Pars*a*iy, for Pars*a*i.

NOTE 1. An exception seems to be adari (NRa).

NOTE 2. H*a*u retains the v even before ci, m*a*i, and t*a*i; e g. h*a*uvci (I). Also occur p*a*ruvnam, p*a*ruvz*a*nanam.

6. Final **a** is sometimes made short before an enclitic; thus, av*a*d*a*shim, for av*a*dashim; m*a*n*a*ca, for m*a*naca. Many examples remain, however, of the long **a** preserved; thus, utam*a*iy, y*a*thasham, etc.

7. The semivowel is often connected with a preceding consonant by its corresponding vowel; thus, adurujiy*a*, for adurujy*a*.

8. A root is often expanded by vowel-insertion; thus, duruj, for druj (Skt. druh).

9. Every Old Persian word must end in **sh**, **m**, an a-vowel, or a semivowel. Should any other letters stand as finals etymologically, they are dropped; thus aj*a*, for aj*a*nt.

10. The dental **s**, when preceded by any vowel except *a* and **a**, is changed into the lingual **sh**; thus, Dar*a*y*a*vush, aish*a*, (for exceptions cf. isu, us*a*t*a*sh*a*n*a*, V*a*umisa, Nisay*a*): also after **kh**, and sometimes after **r**; thus, khsh*a*p*a*, ad*a*rshn*a*ush, (but t*a*rs*a*tiy, Pars*a*, etc.).

Note. In the root h*a*d (originally s*a*d) the influence of a preceding **i** is felt, even with the augment; thus, niy*a*shad*a*y*a*m.

11. The final **s**, after being changed into **h**, is lost; thus, Pars*a*(h) m*a*rtiya(h).

12. The dental before **t** is changed into **s** (as in Avestan); thus, b*a*st*a*, bound, for b*a*dt*a*.

The semivowel **r** sometimes causes a preceding consonant to become aspirated; thus, c*a*khriya (from k*a*r), Mithr*a*, ufr*a*st*a*m.

14. Final **h** has gone over into the palatal **j** in the root duruj (Skt. druh), the influence of the aspiration being felt only in the form durukht*a*m. This exhibits the treatment of the palatal, namely, that it reverts to its original guttural if followed by any other sound than a vowel.

Note. Final **h** of th*a*h becomes **s** before **t**; thus, th*a*st*a*n*a*iy.

15. Medial **h** has a tendency to fall away; thus, thatiy, for th*a*h*a*tiy; mahya for mah*a*hya, (but Aur*a*m*a*zdah*a*).

PART II.

ETYMOLOGY.

NOUNS AND ADJECTIVES.

CASE ENDINGS.

16. Endings: Singular. A. The usual masculine and feminine ending in the nominative is **s**. Stems in *a* and **a** have allowed the **s** to pass over into **h** (cf. 11) which has dropped away, thus leaving the bare stem. Stems in **i** and **u** retain the **s** in the form **sh** (cf. 10). By consonant forms it is euphonically lost. Neuters(except *a*-stems, which add **m**) show the simple stem in this case. The pronominal ending for this gender is historically **t**, which is dropped at the end of a word, but changed to **sh** before the enclitic ciy. The common ending of the personal pronouns is *a*m (which is found also in the plural).

B. The accusative ends in **m** or *a*m in masculine and feminine nouns. The neuter has the same ending as the nominative.

C. The instrumental ending is **a**. In the pronominal declensions the nasal (**n**) is inserted between the stem and ending.

D. The ablative of *a*-stems doubtless ended in the historical **t** or **d**, which being final has been dropped euphonically (cf. 9). Elsewhere the ablative has the same ending as the genitive.

E. The genitive of *a*-stems adds hya (for original sy*a*). The ending of consonant stems is *a* for *a*h (original *a*s). Masculine stems in **i** and **u** have regularly the historic ending *a*s, the *a* of which combines with the vowel of the stem into *a*i (**ai**) and *a*u, the **s** being preserved in the form **sh** (cf. 10). Feminine stems take the fuller ending, **a** for ah (original as) separated by an interspersed **y**.

F. The locative ending is **i** in consonant and *a*-stems, which appear euphonically in the form iy, *a*iy (cf. 5). In masculine u-stems this case ends in *a*u (euphonically *a*uv for an original *a*vi). If this case occurred in a masculine i-stem, the form would be analogous, i. e., *a*i□(euphonically *a*iy for an original *a*yi). An artificial ending of feminine stems is the addition of **a** to the masculine ending; thus, *a*uva, *a*iya. The true locative ending of this gender appears probably in one or two words in the form **a**, (duv*a*r*a*ya, d*a*st*a*ya? perhaps loc. dual, Arbiraya).

G. The vocative ends in the simple stem.

DUAL: A. The ending of the nominative, accusative, and vocative is **a** as in the Veda.

B. A doubtful form of the locative occurs as **a**, (d*a*st*a*ya.)

PLURAL: A. In the nominative the masculine and feminine ending *a*h*a* appears, (corresponding to the Vedic *a*s*a*s). The shorter ending *a*, *a*h (original *a*s) is also in use. Pronominal *a*-stems have the masculine nominative in *a*i. The neuter stems in *a* end in **a**.

B. The accusative ending is *a* for *a*h (original [*a*]ns) in consonant-stems. In *a*-stems the case appears in the form **a**. Neuter stems have this case like the nominative.

C. The instrumental has everywhere the form bish, uniting with *a*-stems into *a*ibish.

D. In the genitive the ending is am. In stems ending in a vowel, the nasal **n** is inserted, before which a short vowel is lengthened. In pronominal declensions **s** is the inserted consonant, before which *a* becomes *a*i.

E. The locative ending is suva. When preceded by *a* or **a**, the **s** passes over into **h** and is dropped, the form becoming uva. When preceded by other vowels the **s** is preserved, and the ending appears as shuva (cf. 10).

17. The normal scheme of endings is as follows:

	SINGULAR.	DUAL.	PLURAL
N.	s(m)	a?	*a*h*a*, *a* (a)
A.	*a*m. m	a?	*a* (a)
I.	a	—	bish
Ab.	*a*	—	—
G.	*a*, (a)s, hya	a?	am
L.	i(a)	a?	suva, uva

For convenience in comparison the case endings in Sanskrit are added.

	SINGULAR.	DUAL.	PLURAL
N.	s(m)	a(au)	*a*s*a*s, *a*s, (a)
A.	*a*m, m.	a(au)	*a*s, n, (a)
I.	a	bhyam	bhis, ais
D.	e	bhyam	bhy*a*s
Ab.	*a*s, (*a*d)	bhyam	bhy*a*s
G.	*a*s (as) s, sy*a*,	os	am
L.	i (am)au	os	su

DECLENSION I.

18. Stems (masculine and neuter) in *a*. Examples: b*a*g*a*, m., god; h*a*m*a*r*a*n*a*, n., battle.

SINGULAR.		SINGULAR.	
N.	b*a*g*a*	N.	h*a*m*a*r*a*n*a*m
A.	b*a*g*a*m	A.	h*a*m*a*r*a*n*a*m
I.	b*a*ga		
Ab.	b*a*ga		
G.	b*a*g*a*hya		
L.	b*a*g*a*iy		
V.	b*a*ga		

DUAL.

N.A.	b*a*ga? (g*a*usha)
L.	b*a*g*a*ya? (d*a*st*a*ya)

PLURAL		PLURAL.	
N.	b*a*gah*a*, b*a*ga	N.	h*a*m*a*r*a*na
A.	b*a*ga	A.	h*a*m*a*r*a*na
I.	b*a*g*a*ibish		
G.	b*a*ganam		
L.	b*a*g*a*ishuva		

Examples of peculiar forms are:

A. The gen. sing. in hy*a* for hya (G*a*rm*a*pad*a*hy*a*).
B. The abl. sing. in *a* for **a** (d*a*rsh*a*m*a*).
C. The loc. sing. in **y** for iy (dur*a*y).
D. The accusative of d*a*r*a*y*a* is identical with the stem in SZb.

DECLENSION II.

19. Stems (masculine) in **a**. Example: Aur*a*m*a*zda m., Auramazda.

SINGULAR.

N.	Aur*a*m*a*zda
A.	Aur*a*m*a*zdam
G.	Aur*a*m*a*zdaha, or Aur*a*m*a*zdah*a*

DECLENSION III.

20. Stems (masculine) in **i** and **u**. Example of i-stem: C*a*ishpi, m., Caishpis.

	SINGULAR
N.	C*a*ishpish
A.	C*a*ishpim
Ab. G.	C*a*ishp*a*ish, or C*a*ishpaish

Example of u-stem: gathu, m., place.

	SINGULAR.		PLURAL.
N.	gathush	G.	gathunam
A.	gathum		
I.	gathva		
Ab. G.	gath*a*ush		
L.	gath*a*uv		

Note: The genitive singular of Dar*a*y*a*v*a*u is Dar*a*y*a*v*a*haush.

DECLENSION IV.

21. Stems (feminine) in **a**, **i**, and **u**. Example of a-stem: t*a*uma, f., family.

	SINGULAR.		PLURAL.
N.	t*a*uma	G.	t*a*umanam
A.	t*a*umam	L.	t*a*umauva
Ab. G.	t*a*umaya		
L.	t*a*umaya or t*a*um*a*ya		

Example of i-stem: Bumi, f., earth.

	SINGULAR.
N.	bumish
A.	bumim
Ab. G.	bumiya

Note: The ending **sh** of the nominative singular is dropped before the enclitic shim in hiapism (Bh I, 19).

Example of u-stem: d*a*hyu, f., country (perhaps irregular).

	SINGULAR		PLURAL
N.	d*a*hyaush	N.	d*a*hyav*a*
A.	d*a*hyaum or d*a*hyum	A.	d*a*hyav*a*
		G.	d*a*hyunam
L.	d*a*hy*a*uva	L.	d*a*hyushuva

DECLENSION V.

22. Stems in *ar*. Example: fr*a*mat*a*r m., leader.

	SINGULAR
N.	fr*a*mata
A.	fr*a*mataram or fr*a*mat*a*r*a*m
G.	fr*a*matr*a* (pitr*a*)

DECLENSION VI.

23. Stems ending in a consonant.

A. Examples: n*a*pat, m., grandson; vith, m., clan.

	SINGULAR.		PLURAL.
N.	n*a*pa		
A.	n*a*pat*a*m(?)		
I.	n*a*pata(?)		
L	n*a*pati(?)		
A.	vith*a*m		
I.	vitha	I.	vithibish or vith*a*bisḥ
L.	vithi		

B. Stems in *a*n (m*a*n, v*a*n). Examples: Vi(n)-d*a*fr*a*n, m., Vindafra; nam*a*n, n., name; asman, m., heaven; khsh*a*tr*a*pav*a*n, m., satrap.

	SINGULAR.
N.	Vi(n)d*a*fra
A.	Vi(n)d*a*fran*a*m

SINGULAR.

N. nam*a*
A. nam*a*

A. asman*a*m

N. khsh*a*tr*a*pava

c. Stems in *a*s, ish. Examples: r*a*uc*a*s, n., day; h*a*dish, n., site.

	SINGULAR.	PLURAL.
N.	r*a*uc*a*	I. r*a*uc*a*bish
A.	r*a*uc*a*	
N.	h*a*dish	
A.	h*a*dish	

HETEROCLITES.

24. Nouns of other declensions have a tendency to assume forms of declension I. Thus, Khsh*a*yarsh*a*hya for Khsh*a*yarshaha; Dar*a*y*a*v*a*(h)ush*a*hya for Dar*a*y*a*v*a*h*a*ush; bum*a*m for bumim; also n*a*m*a* sometimes takes the form of a feminine noun in a; thus, n*a*ma for n*a*m*a*.

COMPARISON OF ADJECTIVES.

25. The comparative and superlative endings are t*a*r*a* and t*a*m*a*; also iy*a*s and isht*a* make corresponding forms of comparison.

PRONOUNS.

26. The pronouns of the first and second persons are thus declined: ad*a*m, I; tuv*a*m, thou.

N.	ad*a*m	N. v*a*y*a*m
A.	mam (enc. mam)	G. amakh*a*m
Ab.	(enc. m*a*)	
G.	m*a*na (enc. m*a*iy)	

N.	tuv*a*m
A.	thuvam
G.	(enc. t*a*iy, t*a*y, Bh. IV, 11.)

27. The demonstrative pronoun av*a* is declined as follows:

SING.	M.	F.	N
A.	av*a*m	—	av*a* (with enc. ciy, av*a*shciy)
G.	av*a*hya	—	av*a*hya

PLUR	M	F	N.
N.	av*a*iy	ava	—
A.	av*a*iy		
G.	av*a*isham	—	—

28 The declension of the other demonstrative h*a*uv (Skt. asau), that, he; aita (Skt. et*a*t), this; and iy*a*m (Skt., ay*a*m), this, is as follows:

SING	M
N.	h*a*uv

SING	M	F	N	PLUR	M	F	N
N.	iy*a*m	iy*a*m	im*a*	N.	im*a*iy	ima	ima
A.	im*a*m	imam		A.	im*a*iy	ima	ima
I.	ana						
G.	—	ahyaya, or ahiyaya					

SING	M
N.	ait*a*
A.	ait*a*

29. Enclitic forms of the pronoun of the third person are:

SINGULAR.		PLURAL	
A.	shim	A.	shish
G.	sh*a*iy	G.	sham
A.	dim	A.	dish

30. The declension of the relative (hy*a* [Skt. sy*a*] ty*a*m, etc) is as follows:

SING	M	F.	N.	PLUR	M	F.	N
N.	hy*a*	hya	ty*a*	N.	ty*a*iy	—	tya
A.	ty*a*m		—	A.	ty*a*iy	—	—
I.	ty*a*na	—	—	G.	ty*a*isham	ty*a*isham	—

31. The interrogative pronoun occurs only in the vocative (masculine singular) ka.

The indefinite pronoun is formed by adding the neuter of the pronominal stem ci; thus, k*a*sciy, cishciy.

32. The adjective aniy*a*, other, forms its neuter according to the pronominal declension; thus, aniy*a*shciy; its ablative is aniy*a*na, after the analogy of the instrumental. H*a*m*a*, all, has the genitive feminine singular h*a*m*a*hyaya.

VERBS.

33. The scheme of the normal endings of the verb is as follows:

PRIMARY ENDINGS

	ACTIVE.		MIDDLE.	
	SING	PLUR	SING.	PLUR.
1.	mi	m*a*hy	*a*i	—
2.	hy	—	—	—
3.	ti	*a*(n)ti	t*a*i	—

SECONDARY ENDINGS.

1.	*a*m	ma	i	—
2.	(h)	—	—	—
3.	(t), s	*a*(n), sh*a*(n)	ta	*a*(n)ta

IMPERATIVE ENDINGS.

1.	—	—	—	—
2.	(*a*)di	ta	uva	—
3.	tu	—	tam	—

NOTE. The ending of the second person hy appears in the form h*a* before the enclitic dish.

SUBJUNCTIVE MOOD.

34. The mood-sign of the subjunctive is *a*, which is added to the tense-stem. If the tense-stem end in *a*, the combination results in **a**. The inscriptions show the primary endings; thus, ah*a*tity from ah, b*a*vatiy from bu (tense-stem b*a*v*a*).

OPTATIVE MOOD.

35. The inscriptions show ya as the mood-sign of the optative, which takes the regular series of secondary endings. Doubtless the simple **i** was taken by the tense-stems in *a* and by the middle voice. The ya is connected with the stem by the union-vowel **i**.

IMPERATIVE MOOD.

36. The imperative has no mood-sign; it adds its endings directly to the tense-stem.

AUGMENT.

37. The augment is a prefixed *a*. If the tense-stem begin with the vowel **i** (or **u**) the augment combines with it into the strengthened diphthong **ai** (or **au**) instead of the regular *a*i, *a*u.

A. In a few cases the augment appears as **a**; thus, p*a*tiyab*a*r*a*m. It is possible, however, to regard this **a** as the combination of the augment and the prefix **a**.

REDUPLICATION.

38. Old Persian reduplication shows the prefixion to a verb-root of its initial consonant and vowel.

A. A long vowel is made short in the reduplicating syllable; thus, ad*a*da from da.

B. A palatal is substituted for a guttural as the consonant of the reduplicating syllable; thus, c*a*khriya from k*a*r.

THE CONJUGATION-CLASSES.

39. The present system (composed of the indicative, subjunctive, optative and imperative) is divided into the following classes:

I. ROOT-CLASS.

In this class there is no class-sign; the personal endings are added directly to the root, unless there be a mood-sign, as in the subjunctive and optative.

II. REDUPLICATING-CLASS.

In this class the present-stem is formed by prefixing a reduplication to the root.

III. THE NU-CLASS.

This class forms its present-stem by adding the syllable nu, which is strengthened to n*a*u in the singular.

IV. THE NA-CLASS.

The syllable na (in the plural ni) is added to the root to form the present-stem.

V. THE *A*-CLASS.

The present-stem is formed by adding *a* to the root, which (1) is strengthened or (2) remains unchanged.

VI. THE Y*A*-CLASS.

The class-sign is *ya*, which is added to the simple root.

VII. THE *A*Y*A*-CLASS.

This class adds *aya* to the strengthened root.

I. ROOT-CLASS.

40. Example: *ja*n, smite.

PRESENT INDICATIVE.

	ACTIVE.		MIDDLE.	
	SING.	PLUR.	SING	PLUR.
1.	ja(n)miy	ja(n)mahy	janaiy	—
2.	ja(n)hy	—	—	—
3.	ja(n)tiy	jana(n)tiy	ja(n)taiy	—

PRESENT SUBJUNCTIVE.

1.	—	—	—	—
2.	janahy	—	—	—
3.	janatiy	?	janataiy	—

PRESENT OPTATIVE.

1.	janiyam	janiyama	?	—
2.	janiya	—	—	—
3.	janiya	?	janiyata	?

PRESENT IMPERATIVE.

1.	—	—	—	—
2.	ja(n)diy	ja(n)ta	januva	—
3.	ja(n)tuv	—	ja(n)tam	—

IMPERFECT.

1.	ajanam	aja(n)ma	ajaniy	—
2.	aja	—	—	—
3.	aja	ajana(n)	aja(n)ta	ajana(n)ta

The form aitiy, (SZb) from root I shows that the root is strengthened, if it is able, in the three persons of the singular active.

As an example of a root beginning with I, illustrating the heavy augment, the form nijayam (for nijaiam) from root I, 'go,' can be quoted.

The verb ah, be, preserves the original **s** before **t**. Its forms are as follows:

PRESENT INDICATIVE.

	SINGULAR.	PLURAL
1.	amiy	am*a*hy
2.	ahy	—
3.	astiy	h*a*(n)tiy

PRESENT SUBJUNCTIVE.

3. ah*a*tiy

IMPERFECT ACTIVE.

1.	ah*a*m	—
2.	—	—
3.	ah*a*	ah*a*(n)

IMPERFECT MIDDLE.

3. ah*a*(n)ta and ah*a*(n)t*a*

II. REDUPLICATING-CLASS.

41. Example: da, put.
Present Imperative, 3. s., d*a*datuv.
Imperfect, 3. s., ad*a*da.

NOTE. The root sta, stand, takes the vowel i as reduplication, and shortens the stem-vowel; aisht*a*ta.

III. NU-CLASS.

42. Examples: j*a*d, ask; d*a*rsh, dare,
Present Imperative, 2. s., j*a*dn*a*utuv.
Imperfect, 3. s., ad*a*rshn*a*ush.

The verb k*a*r, do, shortens the root to ku in the present and imperfect. Its forms are as follows:

PRESENT SUBJUNCTIVE: SING. PLUR.

2. kun*a*vahy

IMPERFECT.

1. akun*a*v*a*m — akuma (for akunuma)

3. akun*a*ush (in [S], akun*a*sh) — akun*a*v*a*(n)

MIDDLE IMPERFECT:

3. akun*a*v*a*ta (in Bh. I, 12, akuta).

NOTE. The union-vowel *a* sometimes follows nu, which is strengthened to n*a*v; thus, v*a*rn*a*vatiy, kun*a*vahy, for v*a*rn*a*v*a*-*a*-ti, etc.

IV. NA-CLASS.

43. All forms of this class are regular (except Imperf. 1. s., adin*a*m, from di, for adinam); thus,

SINGULAR

1. adin*a*m
2. adina, etc.

V. *A*-CLASS.

44. Examples: gub, call; bu, be; b*a*r, bear; jiv, live.

NOTE In the following classes, the stem-final *a* is lengthened to a before m of the 1st personal endings, but is lost before *a*m of the 1st sing imperf and the 3d pl endings, and the short *a* of the ending remains (or vice versa) The imperative takes no ending (unless it be *a*, which unites with the class-sign into a).

(1.) Examples of the strengthened root (corresponding to the unaccented *a*-class of the Sanskrit) are gub and bu. Roots in u (and i) strengthen their vowel to *a*u (and *a*i) which before the case-sign appears as *a*v (and *a*y).

PRESENT MIDDLE: SING. PLURAL.

3. g*a*ub*a*t*a*iy

PRESENT ACT. SUBJ.

2. b*a*vahy
3. b*a*vatiy

IMPERFECT.

1. ab*a*v*a*m
2. ab*a*v*a*
3. ab*a*v*a* — ab*a*v*a*(n).

(2.) Examples of the unchanged root (corresponding to the accented *a*-class of the Sanskrit) are b*a*r and jiv.

PRESENT ACTIVE SING.	PLURAL.
2. b*a*r*a*hy	
3. b*a*r*a*tiy	b*a*r*a*(n)tiy

PRESENT ACT. SUBJ

2. b*a*rahy
3 b*a*ratiy

IMPERATIVE

2. jiva
3. jiv*a*tuv

IMPERFECT ACTIVE.	
3. ab*a*r*a*	ab*a*r*a*(n)

IMPERFECT MIDDLE	
3. ab*a*r*a*ta	ab*a*r*a*(n)ta

VI. *YA*-CLASS.

45.

NOTE 1 The passive formation is the middle-endings added to the class-sign

NOTE 2 The class sign is often connected with the root by an interposed I

Examples: duruj, deceive; m*a*r, die; th*a*h, say.

A. Examples of the simple class in active are duruj, m*a*r.

PRESENT ACTIVE, SING

1. durujiyamiy

PRES. ACT SUBJ,

2. durujiyahy

IMPERFECT ACTIVE,

3. adurujiy*a*

IMPERFECT MIDDLE,

3. am*a*riy*a*ta

B. Example of the passive formation is th*a*h, which verb adds the active ending in the first person plural.

PRESENT, PLURAL.

1. th*a*hyam*a*hy

NOTE 3. The passive formation of k*a*r, do, is upon the strengthened stem; e. g., Imperf 3 s., akun*a*vy*a*ta.

NOTE 4. It is possible to regard the form ath*a*hy*a* as the imperfect 3d sing, with the active ending, instead of the middle, yet possessed of a passive sense. I prefer to read, however, ath*a*hy, believing it to be the passive aorist with short vowel in the stem. (Cf 50 N)

VII. A*YA*-CLASS.

46.

NOTE 1 A causative conjugation is made from this class, but all verbs belonging to this class have not a causative value

NOTE 2 The class-sign is added to the strengthened root.

Examples: d*a*r, hold; ish, send; sta, stand.

A. Examples of the simple class are d*a*r, and ish.

Present, 1. s., dar*a*yamiy

Imperfect, 3. s., adar*aya*

IMPERFECT, SING.

1. aish*a*y*a*m
2 aish*aya*

B. Example of the causative conjugation is sta.

IMPERFECT, SING.

1. astay*a*m
3. astay*a*

NOTE 3 Sometimes the class-sign appears as ay*a*; thus, ag*a*rbay-*a*m, ag*a*rbay*a*, etc

Verbs sometimes make their formation in more than one class; thus, j*a*diyamiy and j*a*dn*a*utuv.

THE PERFECT.

47. The Old Persian has left us only one example of the perfect; i. e., Optative, 3 s., c*a*khriya from k*a*r.

THE AORIST.

48. There have been preserved two aorists; (1) the root aorist, which adds the personal endings directly to the root, and (2) the sibilant aorist, which takes s*a* as a tense-sign. An example of the root aorist is the form ada, 3d person singular of da. Examples of the sibilant aorist are aish*a*, 3d person sing., and aish*a*(n), 3d person plur. of root I.

49. The aorist adds the secondary endings to the tense-stem, to which the augment has been prefixed.

50. The root-aorist has a peculiar formation, which is passive in meaning, corresponding to what the Hindu grammarians call the "passive aorist" of the Sanskrit. The third person singular of the middle is the only form in use. This person is made by adding i (which it has borrowed from the first person) to the root. Euphonically, the form appears as iy or y. The root is usually strengthened; thus, adariy or adary from d*a*r.

NOTE. In the root th*a*h, the stem-vowel remains short; thus, ath*a*hy (for athahy). The Hindu grammarians mention certain roots of the Sanskrit in *a*m, which preserve the short *a*; thus, ag*a*mi, av*a*dhi, etc.

51. The optative of the root-aorist doubtless appears in ag*a*miya from g*a*m.

NOTE The root bu loses its stem-vowel in this mode; e. g., biya.

FUTURE.

52. The Old Persian has left no future-system. A periphrastic future is built out of a nomen agentis and the auxiliary bu; thus, j*a*ta biya (Bh. IV, 17), let him be a killer; i. e., let him kill (he shall kill).

PASSIVE PARTICIPLE.

53. The passive participle is formed by adding t*a* to the simple root; thus, k*a*rt*a* from k*a*r.

INFINITIVE.

54. The Old Persian infinitive is formed by the suffix t*a*n*a* (Lat. tinus in crastinus, diutinus) which appears always in the locative case; thus, k*a*(n)t*a*-n*a*iy from k*a*n.

NOTE The infinitive of k*a*r changes the initial guttural of the root to a palatal: e. g., c*a*rt*a*n*a*iy.

PREPOSITIONS.

55. With accusative: abiy, ant*a*r, athiy, up*a*riy, upa, p*a*tiy, p*a*tish, p*a*riy.

With instrumental: p*a*tiy, h*a*da.

With genitive: abish, p*a*tiy, p*a*sa.

With ablative: h*a*ca.

With locative; anuv, p*a*tiy.

VERBAL PRFFIXES.

56. atiy—across, beyond
ap*a*—away, forth.
av*a*—down, off.
a—to, unto.
ud, us—up, out.
up*a*—to, towards.
ni—down, into.
nij—out, forth.
p*a*ra—away, forth.
fr*a*—forward, forth.
h*a*m—together.

PRIMARY SUFFIXES.

57. *a*, a, *a*h, i, ish, u, t*a*r (forming nouns of agency and relationship), ti, tu, tha, thi, thu, tr*a*, da, na, m*a*n, ma, ya, yu, r*a*.

SECONDARY SUFFIXES.

58 iy*a*, pertaining to (used also to form the patronymic).

ain*a*, consisting of.

k*a* (an adjectival suffix).

t*a* (having an ablative value and often used for that case).

ta (adverbial suffix).

tha (having a local sense).

da (adverbial suffix).

n*a* (adjectival suffix).

r*a* (adjectival suffix).

v*a*n, 'possessed of.'

PART III.

SYNTAX.

59. Although the Old Persian language can be called syntactical, yet there exist many traces of that loose and free construction (paratax) which is original to speech.

USES OF THE NUMBERS.

60. One or two peculiar constructions call for notice.

A. A collective noun in the singular often has the government of a plural noun, both over a verb and a pronoun; thus, imam bumim......ty*a*sham ad*a*m ath*a*h*a*m av*a* akun*a*v*a*ta (NRa) 'This earth...... what I commanded them (i. e., this earth) this was done.'

B. The singular of the personal pronoun ad*a*m can be expanded in a following clause into the plural; thus, p*a*tish mam h*a*m*a*r*a*n*a*m c*a*rt*a*n*a*iy p*a*sav*a* h*a*m*a*r*a*n*a*m akuma (Bh. I, 19) 'to engage in battle against me, afterwards we engaged in battle.'

C. The plural can be used for the dual; thus, av*a*thasham h*a*m*a*r*a*n*a*m k*a*rt*a*m (Bh. II, 6) 'thus the battle was fought by them.' (i. e., the army of Vidarna and the rebellious army); Anam*a*k*a*hy*a* mahya II r*a*uc*a*bish (Bh. I, 19) 'on the 2d day of the month Anamaka' (lit., with two days).

USES OF THE CASES.

THE NOMINATIVE.

61. The nominative is the case of the subject of a finite verb, and of all words qualifying the subject, both attributively, predicatively, and appositionally. A few peculiar uses are to be noticed.

A. The nominative is used often in the weak syntax common to the Old Iranian languages. Artificially it can be explained as the subject of astiy supplied, the idea being repeated in the form of a pronoun; thus, m*a*rtiy*a* Frad*a* nam*a* av*a*m m*a*thisht*a*m akun*a*v*a*(n)ta (Bh. III, 3) 'a man, Frada by name, him they made chief.'

NOTE 1 The pronoun is sometimes omitted, leaving the nominative where the accusative of the direct object would be expected; ad*a*m fraish*a*y*a*m Dad*a*rsis nam*a* Pars*a* m*a*na b*a*(n)d*a*k*a* (Bh III, 2) 'I sent forth my subject, Dadarsis by name, a Persian.'

NOTE 2 This free use of the nominative is shown in such expressions as Kug*a*n*a*k*a* nam*a* v*a*d*a*n*a*m (Bh II, 3) 'there is a town, Kuganaka by name, (lit there is a town, [its] name is Kuganaka) That nam*a* is nominative, not accusative, is shown by the fact that it sometimes agrees in gender with the noun, if that be feminine, e g, Sik*a*ty*a*uv*a*tish nama dida Nishay*a* nama d*a*hyaush (Bh I, 13) 'there is a stronghold, Sikatyauvatis by name, there is a country, Nishaya by name.'

B. The nominative is used in the predicate after a verb in the middle voice which has the force of a passive; thus, hy*a* N*a*buk(u)dr*a*c*a*r*a* ag*a*ub*a*ta (Bh. I, 19) 'who called himself (i. e. was called) Nabukudracara.'

THE VOCATIVE

62. The vocative is the case of direct address.

The following peculiarity needs to be considered, namely: The vocative of the personal pronoun tuv*a*m is made indefinite by the insertion of the interrogative ka in the same case; thus, tuv*a*m ka hy*a* ap*a*r*a*m imam dipim̐ v*a*inahy (Bh. IV, 15) 'O thou (whoever thou art) who wilt hereafter see this inscription.'

THE ACCUSATIVE.

63. The accusative is the case of the direct object of a verb, and of all words which qualify the object, both attributively, predicately, and appositionally; e. g. Aur*a*m*a*zda hy*a* imam bumim ada (O.) 'Auramazda who created this earth.'

64. Some verbs which allow two constructions may take two accusatives, one in each construction; e. g., verbs of asking, taking, etc.; as ait*a* ad*a*m Aur*a*m*a*zdam j*a*diyamiy (NRa.) 'I beg this of Auramazda.' khsh*a*tr*a*mshim ad*a*m adin*a*m (Bh. I, 13). 'I took the kingdom from him.'

A. The verbs k*a*r and da admit two accusatives, one as object, the other as predicate; thus, hy*a* Dar*a*-*yava*(h)um khshay*a*thiy*a*m akun*a*us. (O.) 'who made Darius king;' h*a*uv Dar*ayava*(h)um khshay*a*thiy*a*m ad*a*da (H.), 'he has made Darius king.'

B. A few verbs strengthen the verbal notion by adding their past passive participle, which becomes an accusative in agreement with the direct object; thus, av*a*m (h)ub*a*rt*a*m ab*a*r*a*m (Bh. I, 8) 'I supported him well; (lit, him well supported I supported.)'

65. The accusative can follow nouns which have such a verbal character that they share the construction of a verb; thus, Aur*a*m*a*zda thuvam d*a*usta biya (Bh. IV, 16) 'may Auramazda be a friend to you.'

66. The accusative stands as the limit of motion, both with and without a preposition; thus, y*a*tha mam kam*a* (Bh. IV, 4) 'as the wish (came) to me' (i. e. as my wish was); ad*a*m (kar*a*m) fraish*ayam* Uv*a*jam, (Bh. I, 17) 'I sent an army to Susiana;' K*a*(m)bujiy*a* Mudrayam ashiy*a*va (Bh. I, 10) 'Cambyses went to Egypt;' (kar*a*m) fraish*aya* abiy Vivan*a*m (Bh. III, 9) 'he sent the army to Vivana.'

67. The accusative expresses extent and duration, both with and without a preposition; thus, khsh*a*pava r*a*uc*a*p*a*tiva av*a* akun*a*v*a*y*a*ta (Bh. I, 7) 'this was done day and night.'

A. The time in which an action took place seems to have been expressed at times by the accusative. One case occurs in the inscriptions; G*a*rm*a*p*a*d*a*hy*a* mahya I r*a*uc*a* th*a*k*a*ta ah*a* av*a*thasham h*a*m*a*r*a*n*a*m k*a*rt*a*m (Bh. III, 1.) 'on the first day of the month Garmapada then it was that thus the battle was fought by them.' This idiom appears occasionally in Sanskrit.

68. The accusative of specification defines the application of a noun; thus, h*a*ca Pirav*a* nam*a* r*a*ut*a* (SZb.) 'from a river, the Nile by name.' Cf. 61, A. n. 2.

THE INSTRUMENTAL

69. The instrumental is the case denoting association and accompaniment originally, and as a derived notion, instrument and means.

70. The instrumental of accompaniment usually takes the preposition h*a*da; thus, aish*a* h*a*da kara (Bh. I, 19) 'he went with his army.'

A. In enumeration the instrumental may be used in the sense of association, when the same case as the preceding nouns would be expected; thus abac*a*ris g*a*ith*a*mca maniy*a*mca v(i)thibishca ....avastay*a*m (Bh. I, 14) 'I restored the commerce and the cattle and the dwellings and together with the clans' (i. e., and the clans.)

71. The instrumental of means or instrument is very frequent; thus, v*a*shna Aur*a*m*a*zdah*a* (Bh. I, 5.) 'by the grace of Auramazda.' ard*a*stan*a* ....vithiya k*a*rt*a* (L.) 'the lofty structure was made by the clan.'

72. The prosecutive instrumental denotes the association of time with an event; thus, Viy*a*khn*a*hya mahya XIV r*a*uc*a*bish th*a*k*a*ta ah*a* y*a*diy ud*a*pat*a*ta

(Bh. I, 11) 'on the 14th day of the month Viyakhna, then it was when he rose up (lit. in connection with 14 days).' Cf. 67, A.

73. The instrumental is sometimes used in the sense of the locative, denoting the point in space; thus, ad*a*mshim gathva avastay*a*m (Bh. I, 14) 'I put it in its place.' m*a*na data ap*a*riyay*a*(n) (Bh. I, 8) 'they followed in my law.' v*a*siy aniy*a*sciy n*a*ib*a*m k*a*rt*a*m ana Parsa (D.) 'there is many another beautiful work in this Persia.'

THE DATIVE

74. The dative case has no existence in Old Persian, its place being taken by the genitive.

THE ABLATIVE.

75. The use of the ablative is to express separation or distinction. The preposition h*a*ca is usually joined to this case.

76. The ablative denotes issue, removal, release, and like relations; thus, khsh*a*tr*a*m ty*a* h*a*ca amakh*a*m t*a*umaya p*a*rab*a*rt*a*m ah*a* (Bh. I, 14) 'the kingdom which was taken from our family.' h*a*uv h*a*cam*a* h*a*mitriy*a* ab*a*v*a* (Bh. III, 5) 'he became estranged (rebellious) from me.'

A. The notion of this ablative passes over to that of cause; thus, kar*a*shim h*a*ca d*a*rsham*a* at*a*rs*a* (Bh. I, 13) 'the state feared him on account of (his) violence.'

77. The ablative expresses defense, which is a development of the idea of removal; thus, h*a*ca dr*a*uga p*a*tip*a*y*a*uva (Bh. IV, 5) 'protect yourself from deceit.' imam d*a*hyaum Aur*a*m*a*zda patuv h*a*ca h*a*inaya h*a*ca d(u)shiyara h*a*ca dr*a*uga (H.) 'may Auramazda protect this province from an army, from failure of crops, and from deceit.'

A. The ablative follows t*a*rs, to fear. Such an ablative contains this same idea of removal (i. e., recoil from a dread object). h*a*ca aniy*a*na ma t*a*rs*a*m (I) 'let me not fear a foe.'

78. The ablative is the case of comparison. This use is simply a special application of its original notion of distinction; thus, ap*a*t*a*r*a*m h*a*ca Parsa (NRa) 'another than a Persian' (lit. another from a Persian.)

THE GENITIVE.

79. The true use of the genitive is to qualify a noun with the same powers as the adjective enjoys. The genitive, however, did not remain restricted to this adjectival construction, but is employed with verbs and adjectives.

80. The subjective genitive, including the author and possessor, expresses the subject of the action; thus v*a*shna Aur*a*m*a*zdah*a* ad*a*m khshay*a*thīy*a* amiy (Bh. I, 5) 'by the grace of Auramazda, I am king.'

A. The genitive regularly follows k*a*rt*a*m, perhaps on account of a substantive idea in the participle; thus, av*a*thasham h*a*m*a*ran*a*m k*a*rt*a*m (Bh. III, 10) 'thus the battle was fought by them.'

NOTE. The genitive expressing means is found in Sanskrit.

B. The genitive follows p*a*sa; thus, kar*a* Pars*a* p*a*sa m*a*na ashiy*a*v*a* (Bh. III, 6) 'The Persian army followed me.'

C. The genitive expresses manner; thus, h*a*m*a*-hyaya th*a*rd*a* (Bh. IV, 7) 'in every way.'

81. The partitive genitive denotes the whole of which a portion is taken; thus, ad*a*m Dar*a*y*a*v*a*(h)ush khshay*a*thiy*a* khshay*a*thiyanam (Bh. I, 1) 'I am Darius, the king of kings.'

A. The genitive is dependent on an adjective (especially a superlative) which has substantival character enough to allow a partitive construction; thus Auramazda hya mathishta baganam (F.) 'Auramazda, who is the greatest of the gods.'

82. The objective genitive, which designates the noun as the object of the action, occurs nowhere in the inscriptions.

83. The datival genitive expresses the indirect object; thus, karahya avatha athaha (Bh. I, 16) 'thus he said to the state.' Auramazda khshatram mana frabara (Bh. I, 5) 'Auramazda gave the kingdom to me.'

NOTE. This use is simply a pregnant construction of the possessive genitive; e g, khshatram mana frabara, he gave the kingdom to me (made it mine by giving). This same power of the genitive is shared by the Prakrit and the late Sanskrit

A. The verb duruj, "to deceive,' is followed by the genitive once in the inscriptions; elsewhere it governs the accusative. Karahya avatha adurujiya Bh. I, 11 'thus he deceived the people.'

B. The genitive enclitic sham follows ajanam in place of the accusative of direct object in Bh. IV, 2 adamsham ajanam, 'I smote them,' and patiyakshaiy NRa.

THE LOCATIVE

84. The locative is the case denoting location and condition. The locative expresses situation, both with and without a preposition; thus, adam khshayathiya Parsaiy (Bh. I, 1) 'I am king in Persia.' hya Madaishuva mathishta aha Bh. II; 6 'who was greatest among the Medes.' vardanam anuv Ufratauva (Bh. I, (19) 'a town on the Euphrates.'

A. The locative takes the place of the instrumental in the expression nipadiy, 'on foot;' e.g., atiyaisha.

*pa*sav*a* Vivan*a* h*a*da kara nip*a*diy (Bh. III, 11) 'afterwards Vivana followed with his army on foot.'

B. The locative can take the place of the partitive genitive; thus, Mad*a*ishuv*a* m*a*thishta (Bh. II, 6) 'the greatest among the Medes.'

THE PECULIARITIES OF THE INSCRIPTIONS OF ARTAXERXES MNEMON AND ARTAXERXES OCHUS.

85. These inscriptions exhibit such careless irregularities that they call for special treatment.

A. The nominative is attracted into the case of the preceding noun, although the predicate appears in the nominative; thus, thatiy Art*a*khsh*a*tra Dar*a*y*a*v*a*(h)ush*a*hya khshay*a*thiy*a*hya putr*a* Dar*a*y*a*v*a*(h)ush*a*hya Artakhsh*a*thrahya khshay*a*thiy*a*hya putr*a* (S.) 'says Artaxerxes, the son of Darius, the king; Darius (was) the son of Artaxerxes, the king.'

B. The nominative appears for the accusative with a qualifying pronoun in the accusative; im*a*m ap*a*dan*a* (S.) '(Darius made) this structure.'

C. The genitive is attracted into the case of the subject or the predicate nominative and appears in the nominative; thus, Art*a*khsh*a*tra Dar*a*y*a*v*a*(h)ush khshay*a*thiy*a* putr*a* (P.) 'Artaxerxes, son of Darius, the king.'

D. The nominative is thrust into the accusative, yet the passive construction is retained; thus, im*a*m usat*a*sh*a*nam atha(n)g*a*nam mam upa mam k*a*rta (P.) 'this stone lofty structure was built by me for myself.'

E. The accusative expresses means, taking the place of the regular genitive construction after k*a*rt*a*m; thus, ty*a* mam k*a*rta (P.) 'what was done by me.'

F. A substantive in the singular takes its participle in the plural; thus, ty*a* mam k*a*rta (P.) 'what was done by me.'

THE ADJECTIVE.

86. The adjective and the participle agree with the substantive in gender, number, and case.

A few peculiar cases are to be noticed.

A. The adjective can be hardened into a neuter substantive and in this way enter into the relation of an appositive or a predicate noun; thus, ciy*kar*a*m* ava *d*ahyav*a* (NRa.) 'beautiful are the regions (lit. a beauty these regions are). h*a*uv k*a*m*a*n*a*m ah*a* (Bh. II, 6) 'that was faithful (lit. a faithful·thing).'

B. The adjective is used, most often in the singular, to take the place of the name of a country; thus, Pars*a*, 'Persia (lit. Persian).' Mad*a*, Media (lit. Median).'

NOTE 1. Sometimes the plural occurs, and in a few cases alternates with the singular; thus, Y*a*una and Yaun*a* (NRa) 'Ionia (lit. Ionian and Ionians).'

NOTE 2. The real name of the country appears a few times; thus, Uvar*a*zmish (NRa.), H*a*r*a*uv*a*tish (Bh. I, 6).

C. The noun vith, 'clan,' when used appositionally takes the place of the regular adjective vithiy*a*; thus, h*a*da v(i)thibish b*a*g*a*ibish (H.) 'with (his) fellow gods (lit. with the gods [namely his] fellows).'

D. In the inscriptions of Artaxerxes Ochus the masculine of the pronoun agrees with the feminine noun; thus, im*a*m us*a*t*a*sh*a*nam (P.) 'this lofty structure.'

PRONOUNS.

87. The demonstrative pronouns av*a* and h*a*uv supply the place of the third personal pronoun.

88. The relative pronoun ty*a*, beside enjoying its ordinary functions, has the following important uses

A. The relative pronoun frequently serves to connect the noun with whatever qualifies it, either appositionally, adjectively, adverbially, genitively, or locatively. In this capacity its independent character is lost and it agrees with its antecedent, not only in gender and number but also in case, thus becoming the equivalent of the Greek article; thus, v(i)th*a*m tyam amakh*a*m (Bh. I. 14) 'the clan of ours.' ty*a*na m*a*na data (Bh. I, 8) 'in my law.' khsh*a*tr*a*m ty*a* Babir*a*uv (Bh. I, 16) 'the kingdom at Babylon.' kar*a*m ty*a*m Mad*a*m (Bh. II, 6) 'the Median army.' Nabuk(u)dr*a*c*a*r*a* amiy hy*a* Nabunit*a*hya putr*a* (Bh. II, 16) 'I am Nabukudracara the son of Nabunita.'

B. The relative can be used in the place of a demonstrative; thus, kar*a*m fr*a*ish*a*y*a*m ty*a*ip*a*tiy (Bh. II, 13) 'I sent an army against these.'

USES OF THE VOICES.

89. There are (as in Sanskrit) two voices, active and middle. The passive notion is conveyed through the middle voice by means of a definite class-sign.

One or two peculiar constructions call for notice.

A. The active with direct object can take the place of the middle; thus, thuvam maty*a* durujiyahy (Bh. IV, 6) 'do not deceive yourself.'

B. The middle without the passive sign sometimes contains the passive signification; thus, hy*a* N*a*buk(u)dr*a*c*a*r*a* ag*a*ub*a*ta (Bh. I 19) 'who was called (lit. called himself) N*a*bukudracara.' ag*a*rbay*a*ta (Bh. II, 13) 'he was taken.' an*a*yata (Bh. I, 17) 'he was led.'

C. The passive participle of neuter verbs has no passive notion, but simply an indefinite past tense; thus h*a*(n)gm*a*ta (Bh. II, 7) 'having come together.'

USES OF THE MOODS.

THE INDICATIVE

90. The indicative is used in the recital of facts.

THE SUBJUNCTIVE

91. The subjunctive has a general future meaning, denoting what is possible and probable. This use is perhaps the historic one from which the nicer and more elaborate values of this mood in the cognate languages have been developed; thus, tuv*a*m ka hy*a* ap*a*r*a*m imam dipim p*a*tip*a*rsahy (Bh. IV, 6) 'O thou who wilt hereafter examine this inscription.'

A. Conditional sentences introduced by y*a*diy, 'if', take their verbs in the subjunctive; thus y*a*diy av*a*tha m*a*niyahy (Bh. IV, 5) 'if thus thou thinkest.'

B. Purpose clauses introduced by y*a*tha, 'in order that', take their verbs in the subjunctive; thus, y*a*tha khshnasahy (NRa.) 'in order that you may know.'

C. The negative maty*a* (ma and ty*a*) denoting purpose or warning takes the subjunctive; thus, maty*a* mam khshnasatiy (Bh. I, 13) 'that (the state) may not know me.'

D. The subjunctive with the negative maty*a* is used to express prohibition, less peremptory than the imperative, more so than the optative; thus, p*a*tik*a*ra maty*a* vis*a*nahy (Bh. IV, 15) 'thou shalt not destroy (these) pictures.'

E. The temporal conjunction yava takes the subjunctive in its ordinary future sense; thus, yava t*a*uma ah*a*tiy (Bh. IV, 16) 'as long as (thy) family shall be.'

THE OPTATIVE.

92. The optative denotes what is desired, in which capacity it is the equivalent of a mild imperative. In a weakened sense it denotes what may or can be.

A. The optative with the negative particle ma expresses a desired negation, not direct prohibition; thus, utat*a*iy t*a*uma ma biya (Bh. IV, 11) 'may there not be a family of thine.'

THE IMPERATIVE.

93. The imperative expresses a command or a desire; thus, p*a*r*a*idiy av*a*m j*a*diy (Bh. II, 7) 'go, smite that (army).'

THE INFINITIVE.

94. The infinitive, in its fundamental and usual sense, expresses purpose, as the dative infinitive of the Veda. It has also become employed in a freer sense as the simple complement of a verb; thus, ais*a* h*a*da kara p*a*tish mam h*a*m*a*r*a*n*a*m c*a*rt*a*n*a*iy (Bh. I, 19) 'he went with (his) army against me to engage in battle,' k*a*sciy n*a*iy ad*a*rshn*a*ush cisciy th*a*st*a*n*a*iy p*a*riy G*a*umat*a*m (Bh. I, 13) 'no one dared to say anything against Gaumata.'

USES OF THE TENSES.

95. A few peculiar uses deserve notice.

A. The present with duvitat*a*r*a*n*a*m denotes that the action was begun in the past and continues in the present. This peculiarity is to be compared with the Latin use of the present with iam diu, etc.

B. The indicative forms of the imperfect and aorist appear without augment. With the loss of this augment the imperfect and aorist sacrifice their own peculiar character and take on other notions. After ma prohibitive the sense is that of a subjunctive or optative; thus, h*a*ca aniy*a*na ma t*a*rs*a*m (I.) 'may I not fear an enemy.'

C. Yata in the sense of "while" takes the imperfect; in the sense of "until" it takes either the imperfect or aorist.

D. The passive participle, both with and without an auxiliary verb, is used in the sense of a passive perfect; thus, amata am*a*hy (Bh. I, 3) 'we have been tested (or prolonged).' B*a*rdiy*a* av*a*j*a*t*a* (Bh. I, 10) 'Bardiya was slain.'

DEPENDENT CLAUSES.

96. Final Clauses. Cf. 91, B. and C.

97. Consecutive Clauses. Ty*a* (the neuter of the relative) introduces clauses expressing result, and takes the verb in the indicative; thus, dr*a*ug*a*dish h*a*mitriya akun*a*ush ty*a* im*a*iy kar*a*m adurujiy*a*sh*a*(n) (Bh. IV, 4) 'a lie made them rebellious so that they deceived the people.'

98. Conditional Clauses. Cf. 91, A.

99. Causal Clauses. Y*a*tha expressing cause takes the verb in the indicative; thus, Aur*a*m*a*zda up*a*stam ab*ara*......y*a*tha n*a*iy arik*a* ah*a*m (Bh. IV, 13) 'Auramazda gave aid, because I was not unfriendly.'

100. Temporal Clauses.

A. Y*a*tha, "while," takes the indicative; "in order that," the subjunctive.

B. Yata, Cf. 95, C.

C. Yava, "as long as," prefers the subjunctive. Cf. 91, E.

INDIRECT DISCOURSE.

101. A form of indirect narrative is hardly developed in the language. Statements are expressed

usually in the most simple direct manner; thus, *yadiy avatha maniyahy dahyaushmaiy* duruva ah*a*tiy (Bh. IV, 5) 'if thus thou thinkest, may my country be safe.'

A. This influence of the direct form of statement is felt often by the pronoun in a dependent clause; thus, kar*a*m avaj*a*niya maty*a*man khshnasatiy (Bh. I, 13) 'he would smite the people that they may not know him (lit. that they may not know me)'; the idea being expressed as it was conceived in the mind of the author.

B. A tendency towards indirect discourse is manifested by the use of the neuter of the relative ty*a*; thus, kar*a*hya n*a*iy azda ab*ava* ty*a* B*a*rdiy*a* av*a*j*a*t*a* (Bh. I, 10) 'there was ignorance on the part of the state that Bardiya was slain.'

Note The relative pronoun y*a*t in Sanskrit appears to have a few times this same function. I refer to a case I have met recently in my reading, namely in the Khandogya Upanishad.

COMPOUNDS.

102. Copulative. The composition of two nouns in coordinate construction as if connected by the conjunction "and" does not appear in the inscriptions.

103. Determinative. The composition of two words, the former of which qualifies the second, either as a noun in case relation, adjective, or verb, occurs; thus, *sarastibara*, 'having bows', Aur*a*m*a*zda, as*a*b*ara*, etc.

104. Adjective. The determinative compound by assuming the idea of "possessing" becomes an adjective; thus, Art*a*khsh*a*tr*a*, 'Artaxerxes' (as a determi-

native, 'lofty kingdom'; as an adjective compound, "'possessing a lofty kingdom'.) zur*a*k*a*r*a*, 'possessing power as action', (h)uv*a*sp*a*, p*a*ruz*a*n*a*, etc.

NOTE. The compound p*a*ruz*a*na has its two members separated, yet preserves the meaning and value of a compound; thus, p*a*ruv z*a*nanan (Ca) (Cb) (K).

102. Prepositional. The composition of two words, the former of which is a preposition governing the second, is found often; thus, p*a*sav*a*, 'after this', t*a*r*a*d*a*r*a*y*a* p*a*tip*a*d*a*m fr*a*h*a*rv*a*m, etc.

VERB-FORMS.

A complete classification of all the verb-forms ocring in the Old Persian language,

Aj (?), drive. (See vocabulary.)

Impf. 3. s., aj*ata*.

Akhsh (?), see. (See vocabulary.)

Impf. I. s., akhsh*a*iy.

Ah. be.

Pres. I. s., amiy; 2. s., ahy, 3. s., astiy; 1. p.; am*a*hy: 3. p., h*a*(n)tiy; 3. s., ah*a*tiy(subj.). Impf. I. s., ah*a*m; 3. s., ah*a*; 3. p., ah*a*(n); 3. p. (middle) ah*a*(n)ta, (ah*a*[n]t*a*).

Av*a*h, ask aid.

Impf. (middle) I. s., av*a*h*a*iy.

I, go.

Pres. 3. s., aitiy; 2. s., idiy (impv.); 2. p.; ita (impv.) Impf. I. s., ay*a*m, 3 p., ay*a*(n). Aor. 3. s., aish*a*; 3. p., aish*a*(n). Part., it*a*

Ish, send.

Impf. I. s, aish*a*y*a*m 3. s., aish*aya*.

K*a*n, dig.

Pres. 3. s., k*a*(n)tuv (impv.). Impf. I. s., ak*a*n*a*m; 3. s., ak*a*. Aor. (passive) 3. s., ak*a*niy. Inf. k*a*(n)t*a*n*a*iy.

K*a*r, do.

Pres. 2. s., kun*a*vahy (subj.), k*a*rahy (subj.) 2. s. k*a*ra (impv.) Impf. I. s., akun*a*v*a*m; 3. s., akun*a*ush, (akunash: S), I. p., akuma, 3. p. akun*a*v*a*(n), 3. s. (middle) akun*a*v*a*ta, 3. p. akun*a*va(n)ta, (akuta), 3. s. (passive) akun*a*vy*a*ta; Perf. 3. s. c*a*khriya (opt.). Inf. c*a*rt*a*n*a*iy; Part k*a*rt*a*.

Khshi (?), rule. (See vocabulary.)

Impf. (middle) 1. s, akhsh*a*iy.

Khshnas, know.

Pres. 2. s. khshnasahy (subj.), 3. s. khshnasatiy (subj.)

G*a*m, go.

Aor. 3. s. gm*a*ta, 3. s. j*a*miya (opt). Part gm*a*t*a*.

G*a*rb, seize.

Impf. 1. s. ag*a*rbay*a*m, 3. s., ag*a*rbay*a*, 3. p. ag*a*rbay*a*(n), 3. s. (middle) ag*a*bay*a*ta,

Gud, hide.

Pres. 2. s. g*a*ud*a*yahy (subj.); Impf. 3, s. ag*a*ud*a*y*a*.

Gub, speak.

Pres. (middle) 3. s. g*a*ub*a*t*a*iy, 3. s. g*a*ubat*a*iy (subj.); Impf. 3. s. ag*a*ub*a*ta.

J*a*d, ask.

Pres. 1. s. j*a*diyamiy, 3. s. j*a*dan*a*utuv (impv.)

J*a*n, smite.

Pres, 2. s. j*a*diy (impv.), 2. p. j*a*ta (impv.) j*a*niya (opt.); Impf. 1 s. aj*a*n*a*m, 3. s. aj*a*, 3 p. aj*a*n*a* (n); Part. j*a*t*a*.

Jiv, live.

Pres. 2. s. jiv*a*hy, 2. s. jiva (impv.)

T*a*khsh, fashion.

Impf. (middle) 1 s. at*a*khsh*a*iy, 3. s. at*a*khsh*a*ta, 3. p. at*a*khsha(n)ta.

T*a*r, cross.

Impf. 1 s. at*a*r*a*(m?) (Bh. V, 4) 3. s., at*a*r*a* (t*a*rtiyana?), 1. p. at*a*r*a*yam*a*; Part. t*a*rt*a*.

Tars, fear.

Pres. 3. s. tarsatiy; Impf, 1. s. atarsam, 3. s. atarsa.

Thad, go.(?)

Impf. 2. s. athadaya.

Thah, say.

Pres. 2. s. thahy, 3. s. thatiy, 1. p, (passive) thahyamahy; Impf. 1, s. athaham, 3. s. athaha; Aor. (passive) 3. s. athahi; Inf. thastanaiy.

Trar, guard.

Impf. 1. s. atrarayam.

Dan, flow.

Pres. 3. s. danauvatiy.

Dar, hold.

Pres. 1. s. darayamiy; Impf. 3. s. adaraya; Aor. (passive) 3. s. adariy (adary, adari).

Darsh, dare.

Pres. (middle) 1. s, darshaiy; Impf. 3. s. adarshnaush.

1. Da, know.

Impf. 3, s. adana.

2. Da, put.

Impf. 3. s. adada; Aor. 3. s. ada, adada.

3. Da, give.

Pres. 3. s. dadatuv (impv,)

1. Di, see.

Pres, 2. s. didiy (impv.)

2. Di, take.

Impf. 1. s. adinam, 3. s. adina; Part. dita.

Duruj, deceive.

Pres. 2. s. durujiyahy (subj.;) Impf. 3. s. adurujiya, 3. p. adurujiy*a*sh*a*(n); Part. durukht*a*.

Duv*a*r, make.(?)

Part. duv*a*rt*a*.

Ni, lead.

Impf. 1. s. an*a*y*a*m, 3. s. an*aya*, 3. s. (middle) an*a*-*y*ata.

P*a*t, fall.

Impf. 3. s. (middle) ap*a*t*a*ta.

P*a*rs, examine.

Pres. 2. s. p*a*rsahy (subj.) 3. s. p*a*rsatiy (subj.) p*a*rsa (impv.); Impf. 1. s. ap*a*rs*a*m; Part. fr*a*st*a*.

Pa, protect.

Pres. 2. s. padiy (impv.), 3. s. patuv (impv,,) 2. s. (middle) p*a*y*a*uva (impv.) Part. pat*a*.

Pish, rub.

Impf. I. s. apish*a*m; Inf. pisht*a*n*a*iy; Part. pisht*a*.

B*a*(n)d, bind.

Part. b*a*st*a*.

B*a*r, bear.

Pres. 3. p. b*a*r*a*(n)tiy, b*a*raty*a*?, 3. s. b*a*r*a*tuv (impv.); Impf. 1. s. ab*a*r*a*m, 3. s. ab*a*ra 3. p. ab*a*ra(n), 3. p. (middle) ab*a*r*a*(n)ta; Part. b*a*rt*a*.

Bu, be.

Pres. 3. s. b*a*vatiy (subj.); Impf. 1. s. ab*a*v*a*m, 3. s. ab*a*va, 3. p. ab*a*v*a*(n); Aor. 3. s. biya (Opt.)

M*a*n, think.

Pres. 3. s. maniyatiy (subj.)

M*a*n, remain.

Impf. 3. s. aman*aya*.

Mar, die.

Impf. (middle) 3. s. amariyata.

Ma, measure.

Part. mata.

Rad, leave.(?)

Impf. 2. s. arada.

Ras, come.

Pres, 3. s. rasatiy (subj.); Impf. 1. s. arasam, 3. s. arasa.

Vain, see.

Pres. 2. s. vainahy (subj.) 3. s. (middle) vainataiy; Impf. 3. s. avaina.

Vaj, lead.

Impf. 1. s. avajam.

Var, cause to believe.

Pres. 3. s. varnavatiy (subj.) 3. s. (middle) varnavatam (impv.)

San, destroy.

Pres. 2. s. sanahy (subj.)

Sar, kill.(?)

Impf. (middle) 3. s. asariyata.

Star, sin.

Impf. 2. s. astarava.

Sta, stand.

Impf. 3. s. aishtata, l. s. astayam, 3. s. astaya.

Shiyu, go.

Impf. 1. s. ashiyavam, 3. s. ashiyava, 3. p. ashiyava(n).

Ha(n)j, throw.

Impf. 1. s. aha(n)jam.

Had, sit.

Impf. 1. s. ahadayam.

TRANSLITERATION

OF

THE INSCRIPTIONS.

I.

INSCRIPTION OF CYRUS.

INSCRIPTION OF MURGHAB (M)

[1]Ad*a*m [2]Kurush [3]khshay*a*thiy*a* [4]H*a*kham*a*nishiy*a*.

---

[1]Ad*a*m, 26. [2]Kurush, 16 [3]khshay*a*thiy*a*, 18 [4]H*a*kham*a*nishiy*a*, 58

II.

INSCRIPTIONS OF DARIUS HYSTASPES.

THE INSCRIPTION OF BEHISTAN. (BH.)

1. Ad*a*m Dar*a*y*a*v*a*(h)ush[*] khshay*a*thiy*a* v*a*zr*a*k*a* khshay*a*thiy*a* khshay*a*thiyanam khshay*a*thiy*a* Pars*a*iy khshay*a*thiy*a* [1]d*a*hyunam V(i)shthasp*a*hya putr*a* Arsham*a*hya [2]n*a*pa H*a*kham*a*nishiy*a*. **2.** [3]Thatiy Dar*a*y*a*v*a*(h)ush khshay*a*thiy*a* m*a*na [4]pita V(i)shtasp*a* V(i)shtasp*a*hya pita Arsham*a* Arsham*a*hya pita Ariyaramn*a* Ariyaramn*a*hya pita [C*a*ishpish] [5]C*a*ishpaish pita H*a*kham*a*nish. **3.** Thatiy Dar*a*y*a*v*a*(h)ush khshay*a*thiy*a* av*a*hy*a*radiy v*a*y*a*m H*a*kham*a*nishiya [6]th*a*hyam*a*hy h*a*ca [7]p*a*ruviy*a*t*a* [8]amata [9]am*a*hy h*a*ca p*a*ruviy*a*t*a* [10]hya amakh*a*m [11]t*a*uma khshay*a*thiya ah*a*(n). **4.** Thatiy Dar*a*y*a*v*a*(h)ush khshay*a*thiy*a* VIII m*a*na t*a*umaya ty*a*iy p*a*ruv*a*m khshay*a*thiya ah*a*(n) ad*a*m n*a*v*a*m*a* IX duvitat*a*rn*a*m v*a*y*a*m khshay*a*thiya am*a*hy, **5.** Thatiy Dar*a*y*a*v*a*(h)ush khshay*a*thiy*a* v*a*shna [12]Aur*a*m*a*zdah*a* ad*a*m khshay*a*thiy*a* amiy Aur*a*m*a*zda khsh*a*tr*a*m [13]m*a*na frab*a*r*a*. **6.** Thatiy Dar*a*y*a*v*a*(h)ush khshay*a*thiy*a* [14]ima d*a*hyav*a* tya m*a*na [15]p*a*tiyaish*a*(n) v*a*shna Aur*a*m*a*zdah*a* [16]ad*a*msham khshay*a*thiy*a* ah*a*m Pars*a* (H)uv*a*j*a* Babirush Athura

---

[*] The author not feeling ready to accept the theory of Linder (Literar. Centralblatt, 1880, p. 358) respecting the derivation of the second member of the compound (cf. Spiegel: Die Altpersischen Keilinschriften, 2nd edition) retained the old spelling +vush in his first edition. The otherwise anomalous genitive +v*a*h*a*ush has induced him to transliterate +v*a*(h)ush. See vocabulary.

[1]d*a*hyunam, 21. [2]n*a*pa, 23. [3]thatiy, 15; 39, V. [4]pita, 22. [5]C*a*ishpaish, 20. [6]th*a*hyam*a*hy, 45, B. [7]p*a*ruviy*a*t*a*, 58. [8]amata, 95, D. [9]am*a*hy 40 (end). [10]hya, 30; 87, A. [11]t*a*uma, 21. [12]Aur*a*m*a*zdah*a*, 19. [13]m*a*na, 83. [14]ima, 28. [15]p*a*tiyaish*a*(n), 48. [16]ad*a*msham, 29.

Arabaya Mudraya tyaiy darayahya Sparda Yauna Mada Armina Katapatuka Parthava Zara(n)ka Haraiva Uvarazamiya Bakhtrish Suguda Ga(n)dara Saka Thatagush Harauvatish Maka fraharvam dahyava XXIII. **7.** Thatiy Darayava(h)ush khshayathiya ima dahyava tya mana patiyaisha(n) vashna Auramazdaha mana ba(n)daka aha(n)ta mana [1]bajim [2]abara(n)ta tyasham hacama athahy khshapava raucapativa [3]ava [4]akunavyata. **8.** Thatiy Darayava(h)ush khshayathiya a(n)tar ima dahyava martiya hya agata aha avam [5](h)ubartam abaram hya arika aha avam (h)ufrastam aparsam vashna Auramazdaha ima dahyava tyana mana data apariyaya(n) yathasham hacama [6]athahy avatha [7]akunavyata. **9.** Thatiy Darayava(h)ush khshayathiya Auramazda mana khshatram frabara Auramazdamaiy upastam [8]abara [9]yata ima khshatram [10]adary vashna Auramazdaha ima khshatram [11]darayamiy. **10.** Thatiy Darayava(h)ush khshayathiya ima tya mana [12]kartam pasava yatha khshayathiya abavam Ka(m)bujiya nama Kuraush putra amakham taumaya [13]hauv paruvam ida khshayathiya aha avahya Ka(m)bujiyahya brata Bardiya [14]nama aha hamata hamapita Ka(m)bujiyahya pasava Ka(m)bujiya avam Bardiyam [15]avaja yatha Ka(m)bujiya Bardiyam avaja karahya naiy azda abava tya Bardiya avajata pasava Ka(m)bujiya Mudrayam ashiyava yatha Ka(m)bujiya Mudrayam ashiyava pasava kara arika abava pasava drauga dahyauva vasiy abava uta Parsaiy uta Madaiy uta aniyauva dahyushuva. **11.** Thatiy Darayava(h)ush khshayathiya pasava I martiya Magush aha Gaumata nama hauv udapatata haca Paishiyauvadaya Arakadrish nama kaufa haca

---

[1] bajim, 20. [2] abara(n)ta, 44, 2. [3] ava, 27. [4] akunavyata, 45, N. 3 [5] (h)ubartam, 64, B. [6] athahy, 45, N. 4; 50, N [7] akunavyata, 42. [8] abara, 44 [9] yata, 95 [10] adary, 50. [11] darayamiy, 46. [12] kartam, 53. [13] hauv, 28. [14] nama, 23, B. [15] avaja, 4, a.

avadasha Viyakhnahya mahya XIV [1]raucabish thakata aha yadiy udayatata hauv karahya avatha [2]adurujiya adam Bardiya amiy hya Kuraush putra Ka(m)bujiyahya brata pasava kara haruva hamitriya abava haca Ka(m)bujiya abiy avam ashiyava uta Parsa uta Mada uta aniya dahyava khshatram hauv agarbayata Garmapadahya mahya IX raucabish thakata aha avatha khshatram agarbayata pasava Ka(m)bujiya (h)uvamarshiyush amariyata. **12**. Thatiy Darayava(h)ush khshayathiya aita khshatram tya Gaumata hya Magush [3]adina Ka(m)bujiyam aita khshatram haca paruviyata amakham taumaya aha pasava Gaumata hya Magush adina Ka(m)bujiyam uta Parsam uta Madam uta aniya dahyava hauv ayasta uvaipashiyam akuta hauv khshayathiya abava. **13**. Thatiy Darayava(h)ush khshayathiya naiy aha martiya naiy Parsa naiy Mada naiy amakham taumaya [4]kashciy hya avam Gaumatam tyam Magum khshatram ditam [5]cakhriya karashim haca darshama atarsa karam vasiy avajaniya hya paranam Bardiyam adana avahyaradiy karam avajaniya [6]matyamam khshnasatiy tya adam naiy Bardiya amiy hya Kuraush putra kashciy naiy adarshnaush cishciy thastanaiy pariy Gaumatam tyam Magum yata adam arasam pasava adam Auramazdam patiyavahaiy Auramazdamaiy upastam abara Bagayadaish mahya X raucabish thakata aha avatha adam hada kamanaibish martiyaibish avam Gaumatam tyam Magum avajanam uta tyaishaiy fratama martiya anushiya aha(n)ta Sikayauvatish [7]nama* dida Nisaya nama dahyaush Madaiy avadashim avajanam [8]khshatramshim adam adinam vashna Auramazdaha adam

---

*For forms nama and nama cf. the Grammar, but see Bartholomae, Arische Forsch I, 58; also Thumb, Zeitsch. für vergl. Sprachforsch. (1891)

[1] raucabish, 23 [2] adurujiya, 45. [3] adina, 43 [4] kashciy, 31. [5] cakhriya, 47 [6] matyamam, 101, A [7] nama, 24, 61, A, Note 2 [8] khshatramshim adam adinam, 64

khshayathiya abavam Auramazda khshatram mana frabara. **14.** Thatiy Darayava(h)ush khshayathiya khshatram tya [1]haca amakham taumaya parabartam aha ava adam patipadam akunavam adamshim [2]gathva* avastayam yatha paruvamciy avatha adam akunavam ayadana tya Gaumata hya Magush viyaka adam niyatrarayam karahya abacarish gaithamca maniyamca [3]v(i)thibishca tyadish Gaumata hya Magush adina adam karam gathva avastayam Parsamca Madamca uta aniya dahyava yatha paruvamciy avatha adam tya parabartam patiyabaram vashna Auramazdaha ima adam akunavam adam hamatakhshaiy yata v(i)tham tyam amakham gathva avastayam yatha paruvamciy avatha adam hamatakhshaiy vashna Auramazdaha yatha Gaumata hya Magush v(i)tham tyam amakham naiy parabara. **15.** Thatiy Darayava(h)ush khshayathiya ima tya adam akunavam pasava yatha khshayathiya abavam. **16.** Thatiy Darayava(h)ush khshayathiya yatha adam Gaumatam tyam Magum avajanam pasava I martiya Atrina nama Upadara(n)mahya putra hauv udapatata (H)uvajaiy karahya avatha athaha adam (H)uvajaiy khshayathiya amiy pasava (H)uvajiya hamitriya abava(n) abiy avam Atrinam ashiyava(n) hauv khshayathiya abava (H)uvajaiy uta I martiya Babiruviya Naditabira nama Aina - - hya putra hauv udapatata Babirauv karam avatha adurujiya adam Nabuk(u)dracara amiy hya Nabunitahya putra pasava kara hya Babiruviya haruva abiy avam Naditabiram ashiyava Babirush hamitriya abava khshatram tya Babirauv hauv agarbayata. **17.** Thatiy Darayava(h)ush khshayathiya pasava adam (karam) [4]fraishayam

---

*** It is possible to regard this form as a locative (gathava) with postpositive a (cf. note on (H)ufratauva I, 19; but the instrumental seems preferable).**

[1] haca amakham taumaya, 76. [2] gathva, 73. [3] v(i)thibishca, 70, A. [4] fraishayam (H)uvajam, 66.

(H)uvajam hauv Atrina basta anayata abiy mam adamshim avajanam. **18.** Thatiy Darayava(h)ush khshayathiya pasava adam Babirum ashiyavam abiy avam Naditabiram hya [1]Nabuk(u)dracara agaubata kara hya Naditabirahya Tigram adaraya‸aishtata uta abish naviya aha pasava adam karam–makauva avakanam aniyam dashabarim akunavam aniyahya ashm . . . anayam Auramazdamaiy upastam abara vashna Auramazdaha Tigram viyatarayama avada karam tyam Naditabirahya adam ajanam vasiy Atriyadiyahya mahya [2]XXVII raucabish thakata aha avatha hamaranam akuma. **19.** Thatiy Darayava(h)ush khshayathiya pasava adam Babirum ashiyavam athiy Babirum yatha - - - - - - - ayam Zazana nama vardanam [3]anuv (H)ufratauva* avada hauv Naditabira hya Nabuk(u)dracara agaubata aisha [4]hada kara [5]patish mam hamaranam cartanaiy pasava hamaranam akuma Auramazdamaiy upastam abara vashna Auramazdaha karam tyam Naditabirahya adam ajanam vasiy aniya apiya - h - - a . . apishim parabara Anamakahya mahya [6]II raucabish thakata aha avatha hamaranam akuma.

---

*(H)ufratauva The a which occurs at the end of this locative termination is doubtless the prefix a of the Sanskrit For a full discussion of this postpositive a; cf Bezzenbergers Beiträge, XIII; also for the same postpositive a in Avestan, cf Jackson Am. Or. Society Proceedings (1889) and Kuhns Zeitschrift, XXXI Cf. Grammar, 16, F.

[1] Nabuk(u)dracara agaubata, 61, B. [2] XXVII raucabish, 72. [3] anuv (H)ufratauva, 84. [4] hada kara, 70. [5] patish mam – catanaiy, 54. N., 60, B, 94. [6] II raucabish, 60, C.

II.

1. Thatiy Darayava(h)ush hkshayathiya pasava Naditabira hada kamanaibish asbaribish abiy Babirum ashiyava pasava adam Babirum ashiyavam vashna Auramazdaha uta Babirum agarbayam uta avam Naditabiram agarbayam pasava avam Naditabiram adam Babirauv avajanam. 2. Thatiy Darayava(h)ush khshayathiya yata adam Babirauv aham ima dahyava tya hacama hamitriya abava(n) Parsa (H)uvaja Mada Athura Armina Parthava Margush Thatagush Saka. 3. Thatiy Darayava(h)ush khshayathiya I martiya Martiya nama Cicikhraish putra [1]Kuganaka nama vardanam Parsaiy avada adaraya hauv udapatata (H)uvajaiy karahya avatha athaha adam Imanish amiy (H)uvajaiy khshayathiya. 4. Thatiy Darayava(h)ush khshayathiya adakaiy adam ashnaiy aham abiy (H)uvajam pasava hacama - - - - (H)uvajiya avam Martiyam agarbaya(n) hyasham mathishta aha utashim avajana(n). 5. Thatiy Darayava(h)ush khshayathiya I martiya Fravartish nama Mada hauv udapatata Madaiy karahya avatha athaha adam Khshathrita amiy (H)uvakhshatarahya taumaya pasava kara Mada hya v(i)thapatiy aha hacama hamitriya abava abiy avam Fravartim ashiyava hauv khshayathiya abava Madaiy. 6. Thatiy Darayava(h)ush khshayathiya kara Parsa uta Mada hya upa mam aha [2]hauv kamanam aha pasava adam karam fraishayam Vidarna nama Parsa mana ba(n)daka avamsham mathishtam akunavam avathasham athaham-paraita avam karam tyam Madam jata hya mana naiy gaubataiy pasava hauv Vidarna hada kara ashiyava yatha Madam pararasa Ma . . . nama vardanam Madaiy avada hamaranam akunaush hada Madaibish hya Madaishuva mathishta aha hauv adakaiy kamanamciy naiy adaraya Auramazdamaiy upastam abara

---

[1] Kuganaka nama, 61 A, Note 2. [2] hauv kamanam-aha, 86 A.

vashna Auramazdaha kara hya Vidarnahya avam karam tyam hamitriyam aja vasiy Anamakahya mahya VI raucabish thakata aha [1]avathasham hamaranam kartam pasava hauv kara hya mana Ka(m)pada nama dahyaush Madaiy avada mam cita amanaya yata adam arasam Madam. 7. Thatiy Darayava(h)ush khshayathiya pasava Dadarshish nama Arminiya mana ba(n)daka avam adam fraishayam Arminam avathashaiy athaham paraidiy kara hya hamitriya mana naiy gaubataiy avam jadiy pasava Dadarshish ashiyava yatha Arminam pararasa pasava hamitriya [2]ha(n)gmata paraita patish Dadarshim hamaranam cartanaiy .... nama avahanam Armaniyaiy avada hamaranam akunava(n) Auramazdamaiy upastam abara vashna Auramazdaha kara hya mana avam karam tyam hamitriyam .. aja vasiy Thuravaharahya mahya VI raucabish thakata aha avathasham hamaranam kartam. 8. Thatiy Darayava(h)ush khshayathiya patiy duvitiyam hamitriya ha(n)gmata paraita patish Dadarshim hamaranam cartanaiy Tigra nama dida Armaniyaiy avada hamaranam akunava(n) Auramazdamaiy upastam abara vashna Auramazdaha kara hya mana avam karam tyam hamitriyam aja vasiy Thuravaharahya mahya XVIII raucabish thakata aha avathasham hamaranam kartam. 9. Thatiy Darayava(h)ush khshayathiya patiy tritiyam hamitriya ha(n)gmata paraita patish Dadarshim hamaranam cartanaiy U .... ama nama dida Armaniyaiy avada hamaranam akunava(n) Auramazdamaiy upastam abara vashna Auramazdaha kara hya mana avam karam tyam hamitriyam aja vasiy Thaigarcaish mahya IX raucabish thakata aha avathasham hamaranam kartam pasava Dadarshish cita mam amanaya . a . . . yata adam arasam Madam. 10. Thatiy Darayava(h)ush khshayathiya pasava Vaumisa nama

---

[1] avathasbam, 60, c [2] ha(n)gmata, 89, c

Parsa mana ba(n)daka avam adam fraishayam Arminam avathashaiy athaham paraidiy kara hya hamitriya mana naiy gaubataiy avam jadiy pasava Vaumisa ashiyava yatha Arminam pararasa pasava hamitriya ha(n)gmata paraita patish Vaumisam hamaranam cartanaiy - - I - - - nama dahyaush Athuraya avada hamaranam akunava(n) Auramazdamaiy upastam abara vashna Auramazdaha kara hya mana avam karam tyam hamitriyam aja vasiy Anamakahya mahya XV raucabish thakata aha avathasham hamaranam kartam. **11.** Thatiy Darayava(h)ush khshayathiya patiy duvitiyam hamitriya ha(n)gmata paraita patish Vaumisam hamaranam cartanaiy Autiyara nama dahyaush Arminaiy avada hamaranam akunava(n) Auramazdamaiy upastam abara vashna Auramazdaha kara hya mana avam karam tyam hamitriyam aja vasiy Thuravaharahya mahya - iyamanam patiy avathasham hamaranam kartam pasava Vaumisa cita mam amanaya Arminaiy yata adam arasam Madam. **12.** Thatiy Darayava(h)ush khshayathiya pasava adam nijayam haca Babiraush ashiyavam Madam yatha Madam pararasam Kud(u)rush nama vardanam Madaiy avada hauv Fravartish hya Madaiy khshayathiya agaubata aisha hada kara patish mam hamaranam cartanaiy pasava hamaranam akuma Auramazdamaiy upastam abara vashna Auramazdaha karam tyam Fravartaish adam ajanam vasiy Adukanaish mahya XXVI raucabish thakata aha avatha hamaranam akuma. **13.** Thatiy Darayava(h)ush khshayathiya pasava hauv Fravartish hada kamanaibish asbaribish amutha Raga nama dahyaush Madaiy avada ashiyava pasava adam karam fraishayam [1]tyaipatiy Fravartish [2]agarbayata anayata abiy mam adamshaiy uta naham uta gausha uta izavam frajanam utashaiy - - - ma avajam duvarayamaiy

[1] tyaipatiy, 88, B. [2] agarbayata anayata, 89, B.

basta adariy haruvashim kara avaina pasava adam Ha(n)gmatanaiy uzamayapatiy akunavam uta martiya tyaishaiy fratama anushiya aha(n)ta avaiy Ha(n)gmatanaiy a(n)tar didam fraha(n)jam. **14.** Thatiy Darayava(h)ush khshayathiya I martiya Citra(n)takhma nama Asagartiya hauvmaiy hamitriya abava karahya avatha athaha adam khshayathiya amiy Asagartaiy (H)uvakhshatarahya taumaya pasava adam karam Parsam uta Madam fraishayam Takhmaspada nama Mada mana ba(n)daka avamsham mathishtam akunavam avathasham athaham paraita karam tyam hamitriyam hya mana naiy gaubataiy avam jata pasava Takhmaspada hada kara ashiyava hamaranam akunaush hada Citra(n)takhma Auramazdamaiy upastam abara vashna Auramazdaha kara hya mana avam karam tyam hamitriyam aja uta Citra(n)takhmam agarbaya anaya abiy mam pasavashaiy adam uta naham uta gausha frajanam utashaiy - - shma avajam duvarayamaiy basta adariy haruvashim kara avaina pasavashim Arbiraya uzamayapatiy akunavam. **15.** Thatiy Darayava(h)ush khshayathiya ima tya mana kartam Madaiy. **16.** Thatiy Darayava(h)ush khshayathiya Parthava uta Varkana - - - - - va - - - - - Fravartaish - - - - agaubata V(i)shtaspa mana pita h - - - - kara avahar - - - - atara pasava V(i)shtaspa ab - - - - - anushiya - - - aya Vispauz - - tish nama vardanam - - - - - da hamaranam akunava - - - - - - - - - - - - avathasham hamaranam kartam.

III.

1. Thatiy Darayava(h)ush khshayathiya pasava adam karam Parsam fraishayam abiy V(i)shtaspam haca Ragaya yatha hauv kara pararasa abiy V(i)shtaspam pasava V(i)shtaspa ayasta avam karam ashiyava Patigrabana nama vardanam Parthavaiy avada hamaranam akunaush hada hamitriyaibish Auramazdamaiy upastam abara vashna Auramazdaha V(i)shtaspa avam karam tyam hamitriyam aja vasiy Garmapadahya mahya [1]I rauca thakata aha avathasham hamaranam kartam. **2.** Thatiy Darayava(h)ush khshayathiya yasava dahyaush mana abava ima tya mana kartam Parthavaiy. **3.** Thatiy Darayava(h)ush khshayathiya Margush nama dahyaush hauvmaiy hashitiya abava [2]I martiya Frada nama Margava avam mathishtam akunava(n)ta pasava adam [3]fraishayam Dadarshish nama Parsa mana ba(n)daka Bakhtriya khshatrapava abiy avam avathashaiy athaham paraidiy avam karam jadiy hya mana naiy gaubataiy pasava Dadarshish hada kara ashiyava hamaranam akunaush hada Margayaibish Auramazdamaiy upastam abara vashna Auramazdaha kara hya mana avam karam . . tyam hamitriyam aja vasiy Atriyadiyahya mahya XXIII raucabish thakata aha avathasham hamaranam kartam. **4.** Thatiy Darayava(h)ush khshayathiya pasava dahyaush mana abava ima tya mana kartam Bakhtriya. **5.** Thatiy Darayava(h)ush khshayathiya I martiya Vahyazdata nama Tarava nama vardanam Yutiya nama dahyaush Parsaiy avada adaraya hauv duvitiyam udapatata Parsaiy karahya avatha athaha adam Bardiya amiy hya Kuraush putra pasava kara Parsa hya v(i)thapatiy haca yadaya fratarta hauv hacama hamitriya abava abiy avam Vahyazdatam ashiyava hauv khshayathiya abava Parsaiy. **6.** Tha-

---

[1] I rauca, 46, A [2] I martiya Frada – avam, 61, A. [3] fraishayam Dadarshish, 61, A, Note 1.

tiy Darayava(h)ush khshayathiya pasava adam karam Parsam uta Madam fraishayam hya upa mam aha Artavardiya nama Parsa mana ba(n)daka avamsham mathishtam akunavam hya aniya kara Parsa [1]pasa mana ashiyava Madam pasava Artavardiya hada kara ashiyava Parsam yatha Parsam pararasa Rakha nama vardanam Parsaiy avada hauv Vahyazdata hya Bardiya agaubata aisha hada kara patish Artavardiyam hamaranam cartanaiy pasava hamaranam akunava(n) Auramazdamaiy upastam abara vashna Auramazdaha kara hya mana avam karam tyam Vahyazdatahya aja vasiy Thuravaharahya mahya XII raucabish thakata aha avathasham hamaranam kartam. 7. Thatiy Darayava(h)ush khshayathiya pasava hauv Vahyazdata hada kamanaibish asabaribish amutha ashiyava Paishiyauvadam haca avadasha karam ayasta hyaparam aisha patish Artavardiyam hamaranam cartanaiy Paraga nama kaufa avada hamaranam akunava(n) Auramazdamaiy upastam abara vashna Auramazdaha kara hya mana avam karam tyam Vahyazdatahya aja vasiy Garmapadahya mahya VI raucabish thakata aha avathasham hamaranam kartam uta avam Vahyazdatam agarbaya(n) uta martiya tyaishaiy fratama anushiya aha(n)ta agarbaya(n). 8. Thatiy Darayava(h)ush khshayathiya pasava adam avam Vahyazdatam uta martiya tyaishaiy fratama anushiya aha(n)ta Uvadaidaya nama vardanam Parsaiy avadashish uzamayapatiy akunavam. 9. Thatiy Darayava(h)ush khshayathiya hauv Vahyazdata hya Bardiya agaubata hauv karam fraishaya Harauvatim Vivana nama Parsa mana ba(n)daka Harauvatiya khshatrapava abiy avam utasham I martiyam mathishtam akunaush avathasham athaha paraita Vivanam jata uta avam karam hya Darayavahush khshayathiyahya gaubataiy pasava hauv kara ashiya-

[1] pasa mana, 80, B.

va tyam Vahyazdata fraishaya abiy Vivanam hamaranam cartanaiy Kapishakanish nama dida avada hamaranam akunava(n) Auramazdamaiy upastam abara vashna Auramazdaha kara hya mana avam karam tyam hamitriyam aja vasiy Anamakahya mahya XIII raucabish thakata aha [1]avathasham hamaranam kartam. **10.** Thatiy Darayava(h)ush khshayathiya patiy hyaparam hamitriya ha(n)gmata paraita patish Vivanam hamaranam cartanaiy Ga(n)dutava nama dahyaush avada hamaranam akunava(n) Auramazdamaiy upastam abara vashna Auramazdaha kara hya mana avam karam tyam hamitriyam aja vasiy Viyakhnahya mahya VII raucabish thakata aha avathasham hamaranam kartam. **11.** Thatiy Darayava(h)ush khshayathiya pasava hauv martiya hya avahya karahya mathishta aha tyam Vahyazdata fraishaya abiy Vivanam hauv mathishta hada kamanaibish asabaribish ashiyava Arshada nama dida Harauvatiya avapara atiyaisha pasava Vivana hada kara [2]nipadiy tyaiy ashiyava avadashim agarbaya uta martiya tyaishaiy fratama anushiya aha(n)ta avaja. **12.** Thatiy Darayava(h)ush khshayathiya pasava dahyaush mana abava ima tya mana kartam Harauvatiya. **13.** Thatiy Darayava(h)ush khshayathiya yata adam Parsaiy uta Madaiy aham patiy duvitiyam Babiruviya hamitriya abava(n) hacama I martiya Arakha nama Arminiya Han(?)ditahya putra hauv udapatata Babirauv Duban(?)a nama dahyaush haca avadasha hauv udapatata avatha adurujiya adam Nabukudracara amiy hya Nabunitahya putra pasava kara Babiruyiya hacama hamitriya abava abiy avam Arakham ashiyava Babirum hauv agarbayata hauv khshayathiya abava Babirauv. **14.** Thatiy Darayava(h)ush khshayathiya pasava adam karam fraishayam Babirum Vi(n)dafra nama Mada mana ba(n)daka

---

[1] avathasham hamaranam kartam, 80, A. [2] nipadiy, 84, A.

avam mathishtam akunavam avathasham athaham paraita avam karam tyam Babirauv jata hya mana naiy gaubataiy pasava Vi(n)dafra hada kara ashiyava abiy Babirum Auramzdamaiy upastam abara vashna Auramazdaha Vi(n)dafra Babirum agarbaya - - - - - mahya II raucabish thakata aha avatha ava - apatiy asariyata.

IV.

1. Thatiy Darayava(h)ush khshayathiya ima tya mana kartam Babirauv. 2. Thatiy Darayava(h)ush khshayathiya ima tya adam akunavam vashna Auramazdaha aha hamahyaya tharda pasava yatha khshayathiya hamitriya abava(n) adam XIX hamarana akunavam vashna Auramazdaha [1]adamsham ajanam uta IX khshayathiya agarbayam I Gaumata nama Magush aha hauv adurujiya avatha athaha adam Bardiya amiy hya Kuraush putra hauv Parsam hamitriyam akunaush I Atrina nama (H)uvajaiy hauv adurujiya avatha athaha adam khshayathiya amiy (H)uvajaiy hauv (H)uvajam hamitriyam akunaush mana I Naditabira nama Babiruviya hauv adurujiya avatha athaha adam Nabukudracara amiy hya Nabunitahya putra hauv Babirum hamitriyam akunaush I Martiya nama Parsa hauv adurujiya avatha athaha adam Imanish amiy (H)uvajaiy khshayathiya hauv (H)uvajam hamitriyam akunaush I Fravartish nama Mada hauv adurujiya avatha athaha adam Khshathrita amiy (H)uvakhshatarahya taumaya hauv Madam hamitriyam akunaush I Citra(n)takhma nama Asagartiya hauv adurujiya avatha athaha adam khshayathiya amiy Asagartaiy (H)uvakhshatarahya taumaya hauv Asagartam hamitriyam akunaush I Frada nama Margava hauv adurujiya avatha athaha adam khshayathiya amiy Margauv hauv Margum hamitriyam akunaush I Vahyazdata nama Parsa hauv adurujiya avatha athaha adam Bardiya amiy Kuraush putra hauv Parsam hamitriyam akunaush I Arakha nama Arminiya hauv adurujiya avatha athaha adam Nabukudracara amiy hya Nabunitahya putra hauv Babirum hamitriyam akunaush. 3. Thatiy Darayava(h)ush khshayathiya imaiy IX khshayathiya adam agarbayam a(n)tar ima hamarana. 4. Thatiy Dara-

[1] adamsham ajanam, 83, B.

yava(h)ush khshayathiya dahyava ima tya hamitriya abava(n) draugadish akunaush [1]tya imaiy karam adurujiyasha(n) pasava dish Auramazda mana dastaya akunaush yatha [2]mam kama avatha di - - . 5. Thatiy Darayava(h)ush khshayathiya tuvam ka khshayathiya hya aparam ahy [3]haca drauga darsham patipayauva martiya hya draujana ahatiy avam (h)ufrastam parsa yadiy avatha [4]maniyahy dahyaushmaiy duruva ahatiy. 6. Thatiy Darayava(h)ush khshayathiya ima tya adam akunavam vashna Auramazdaha [5]hamahyaya tharda akunavam tuvam ka hya aparam imam dipim [6]patiparsahy tya mana kartam varnavatam [7]thuvam matya durujiyahy. 7. Thatiy Darayava(h)ush khshayathiya Auramazda taiyiya yatha ima hashiyam naiy durukhtam adam akunavam hamahyaya tharda. 8. Thatiy Darayava(h)ush khshayathiya vashna Auramazdaha - - amaiy aniyashciy vasiy astiy kartam ava ahyaya dipiya naiy nipishtam avahyaradiy naiy nipishtam matya hya aparam imam dipim patiparsatiy avahya paruv tha . . . . tya mana kartam naishim varnavatiy durukhtam maniyatiy. 9. Thatiy Darayava(h)ush khshayathiya tyaiy paruva khshayathiya - a aha(n) avaisham naiy astiy kartam yatha mana vashna Auramazdaha hamahyaya duvartam. 10. Thatiy Darayava(h)ush khshayathiya - - - nuram thuvam varnavatam tya mana kartam avatha - - - avahyaradiy ma apagaudaya yadiy imam ha(n)dugam naiy apagaudayahy karahya thahy Auramazda thuvam daushta [8]biya utataiy tauma vasiy biya uta dra(n)gam jiva. 11. Thatiy Darayava(h)ush khshayathiya yadiy imam ha(n)dugam apagaudayahy naiy thahy karahya Auramazdatay jata biya utataiy tauma ma biya. 12. Thatiy Darayava(h)ush khshayathiya ima tya adam akunavam hamahyaya tharda

---

[1] tya imaiy karam adurujiyasha(n), 97. [2] mam kama, 66. [3] haca drauga, 77. [4] maniyahy, 91, A [5] hamahyaya tharda, 80, c. [6] patiparsahy, 91. [7] thuvam matya durujiyahy, 89, A [8] biya, 51, N.

vashna Auramazdaha akunavam Auramazdamaiy upastam abara uta aniya bagaha tyaiy ha(n)tiy. **13.** Thatiy Darayava(h)ush khshayathiya avahyaradiy Auramazda upastam abara uta aniya bagaha tyaiy ha(n)tiy yatha naiy arika aham naiy draujana aham naiy zurakara aham - - - - - imaiy tauma upariy abashtam upariy mam naiy shakaurim - - - - - huvatam zura akunavam tyamaiy hya hamatakhshata mana vithiya avam (h)ubartam abaram hya iyani . . avam (h)ufrastam aparsam. **14.** Thatiy Darayava(h)ush khshayathiya [1]tuvam ka khshayathiya hya aparam ahy martiya hya draujana ahatiy hyava - tar - - - ahatiy avaiy ma daushta avaiy ahifrashtadiy parsa. **15.** Thatiy Darayava(h)ush khshayathiya tuvam ka hya aparam imam dipim vainahy tyam adam niyapisham imaiva patikara matya [2]visanahy yava jivahy ava(?) avatha parikara. **16.** Thatiy Darayava(h)ush khshayathiya yadiy imam dipim vainahy imaiva patikara naiydish visanahy utamaiy [3]yava tauma ahatiy parikarahadish Auramazda [4]thuvam daushta biya utataiy tauma vasiy biya uta dra(n)gam jiva uta tya kunavahy avataiy Auramazda m - - - m jadanautuv. **17.** Thatiy Darayava(h)ush khshayathiya yadiy imam dipim imaiva patikara vainahy visanahadish utamaiy yava tauma ahatiy naiydish parikarahy Auramazdataiy jata biya utataiy tauma ma biya uta tya kunavahy avataiy Auramazda nika(n)tuv. **18.** Thatiy Darayava(h)ush khshayathiya imaiy martiya tyaiy adakaiy avada aha(n)ta yata adam Gaumatam tyam Magum avajanam hya Bardiya agaubata adakaiy imaiy martiya hamatakhsha(n)ta anushiya mana Vi(n)dafrana nama Vayasparahya putra Parsa Utana nama Thukhrahya putra Parsa Gaubaruva nama Marduniyahya putra Parsa Vidarna nama Bagabignahya

---

[1] tuvam ka, 62 [2] visanahy, 91, D. [3] yava tauma ahatiy, 91, E.
[4] thuvam daushta biya, 65.

putr*a* Pars*a* B*a*g*a*bukhsh*a* nam*a* Daduhy*a*hya putr*a* Pars*a* Ardum*a*nish nam*a* V*a*h*a*uk*a*hya putr*a* Pars*a*.

19. Thatiy Dar*ayava*(h)ush khshay*a*thiy*a* tuv*a*m ka khshay*a*thiy*a* hy*a* ap*a*r*a*m ahy tyama vidam t*a*rtiyana—ty*a* Dar*ayava*(h)ush - - - - - - - - - - - - - - - akun*a*v*a*m.

V.

1. Thatiy Darayava(h)ush khshayathiya ima tya adam akunavam ma . r . . . . . . thardam - - tha khshayathiya . . . . vajanam . . . . . . dahyaush hauv hacama hamitriya abava I martiya - imaima nama (H)uvajiya avam mathishtam akunava(n) pasava adam karam fraishayam (H)uvajam I martiya Gaubaruva nama Parsa mana ba(n)daka avamsham mathishtam akunavam pasava hauv Gaubaruva hada kara ashiyava (H)uvajam hamaranam akunaush hada hamitriyaibish pasava . . . . . . utashaiy marda uta . . . . agarbaya uta aniya abiy mam . . . . dahyaush . . . . janam avadashim . . . . **2.** Thatiy Darayava(h)ush khshayathiya a . . . uta dah . . . Auramazda . . aya . . . vashna Auramazdaha . . . thadish akunavam. **3.** Thatiy Darayava(h)ush khshayathiya hya aparam imam ya . . . . . . hatiy uta jivahya . . . . . . **4.** Thatiy Darayava(h)ush khshayathiya . . . . . . ashiyavam abiy Sakam . . . . Tigram baratya . . . . iy abiy darayam avam . . . . a pisa viyatara . . . . ajanam aniyam agarbayam . . . . abiy mam uta . . . . . . Saku(n)ka nama avam agarbayam . . . . avada aniyam mathishtam . . . . am aha pasava da . . . . **5.** Thatiy Darayava(h)ush khshayathiya . . . . ma naiy Auramazda . . . . yadiy vashna Auramazdaha . . . . akunavam. **6.** Thatiy Darayava(h)ush khshayathiya . . . . . . Auramazdam yadata . . . . uta jivahya uta . .

Smaller Behistan Inscriptions.

a.

OVER THE PICTURE OF DARIUS.

Ad*a*m Dar*ayava*(h)ush khshay*a*thiy*a* v*a*zr*a*k*a* khshay*a*thiy*a* khshay*a*thiyan*a*m khshay*a*thiy*a* Pars*a*iy khshay*a*thiy*a* d*a*hyunam V(i)shtasp*a*hya putr*a* Arsham*a*hya n*a*pa H*a*khaman*a*nishiy*a* Thatiy Dar*aya*v*a*(h)ush khshay*a*thiy*a* m*a*na pita V(i)shtasp*a* V(i)shtasp*a*hya pita Arsham*a* Arsham*a*hya pita Ariyar*a*mn*a* Ariyar*a*mn*a*hya pita C*a*ishpish C*a*ishp*a*ish pita H*a*kham*a*nish Thatiy Dar*a*y*a*v*a*(h)ush khshay*a*thiy*a* av*a*hy*a*radiy v*a*y*a*m H*a*kham*a*nishiya th*a*hyam*a*hy h*a*ca p*a*ruviy*a*t*a* amata am*a*hy h*a*ca p*a*ruviy*a*t*a* hya amakh*a*m t*a*uma khshay*a*thiya ah*a*(n) Thatiy Dar*aya*v*a*(h)ush khshay*a*thiy*a* VIII m*a*na t*a*umaya ty*a*iy p*a*ruv*a*m khshay*a*thiya ah*a*(n) ad*a*m n*a*v*a*m*a* IX duvitat*a*rn*a*m v*a*y*a*m khshay*a*thiya am*a*hy

b.

UNDER THE PROSTRATE FORM.

Iy*a*m G*a*umat*a* hy*a* M*a*gush adurujiy*a* av*a*tha ath*a*h*a* ad*a*m B*a*rdiy*a* amiy hy*a* Kur*a*ush putr*a* ad*a*m khshay*a*thiy*a* amiy.

c.

OVER THE FIRST UPRIGHT FIGURE.

Iy*a*m Atrin*a* adurujiy*a* av*a*tha ath*a*h*a* ad*a*m khshay*a*thiy*a* amiy (H)uv*a*j*a*iy.

d.

OVER THE SECOND FIGURE.

Iy*a*m N*a*dit*a*bir*a* adurujiy*a* av*a*tha ath*a*h*a* ad*a*m N*a*buk(u)dr*a*c*a*r*a* amiy hy*a* N*a*bunit*a*hy*a* putr*a* ad*a*m khshay*a*thiy*a* amiy Babir*a*uv.

e.

UPON THE LOWER PART OF THE ATTIRE OF THIRD FIGURE.

Iy*a*m Fr*a*v*a*rtish adurujiy*a* av*a*tha ath*a*h*a* ad*a*m Khsh*a*thrit*a* amiy (H)uv*a*khshay*a*t*a*r*a*hy*a* t*a*umaya ad*a*m khshay*a*thiy*a* amiy Mad*a*iy.

f.

OVER THE FOURTH FIGURE.

Iy*a*m M*a*rtiy*a* adurujiy*a* av*a*tha ath*a*h*a* ad*a*m Im*a*-nish amiy (H)uv*a*j*a*iy khshay*a*thiy*a*.

g.

OVER THE FIFTH FIGURE.

Iy*a*m Citr*a*(n)t*a*khm*a* adurujiy*a* av*a*tha ath*a*h*a* ad*a*m khshay*a*thiy*a* As*a*g*a*rt*a*iy (H)uv*a*khsh*a*t*a*r*a*hy*a* t*a*u-maya.

h.

OVER THE SIXTH FIGURE.

Iy*a*m V*a*hy*a*zdat*a* adurujiy*a* av*a*tha ath*a*h*a* ad*a*m B*a*rdiy*a* amiy hy*a* Kur*a*ush putr*a* ad*a*m khshay*a*thiy*a* amiy.

i.

OVER THE SEVENTH FIGURE.

Iy*a*m Ar*a*kh*a* adurujiy*a* av*a*tha ath*a*h*a* ad*a*m N*a*-buk(u)dr*a*c*a*r*a* amiy hy*a* N*a*bunit*a*hya putr*a* ad*a*m khshay*a*thiy*a* amiy Babir*a*uv.

j.

OVER THE EIGHTH FIGURE.

Iy*a*m Frad*a* adurujiy*a* av*a*tha aṭh*a*h*a* ad*a*m khsha-*ya*thiy*a* amiy M*a*rg*a*uv.

k.

OVER THE NINTH FIGURE.

Iy*a*m S*a*ku(n)k*a* hy*a* Sak*a*.

III.

The Inscription of Alvend. (O.)

B*a*g*a* v*a*zr*a*k*a* Aur*a*m*a*zda hy*a* imam bumim ada hy*a* av*a*m asman*a*m ada hy*a* m*a*rtiy*a*m ada hy*a* shiyatim ada m*a*rtiy*a*hya hy*a* [1]Dar*a*y*a*v*a*(h)um khshay*a*thiy*a*m aiv*a*m p*a*runam fr*a*matar*a*m Ad*a*m Dar*a*y*a*-v*a*(h)ush khshay*a*thiy*a* v*a*zr*a*k*a* khshay*a*thiy*a* khshay*a*thiyanam khshay*a*thiy*a* d*a*hyunam p*a*ruz*a*nanam khshay*a*thiy*a* ahyaya bumiya v*a*zr*a*kaya dur*a*iy apiy Vishtasp*a*hya putr*a* H*a*khama*n*ishiy*a*.

---

[1] Dar*a*y*a*v*a*(h)um khshay*a*thiy*a*m akun*a*ush, 64, A.

IV.

Inscriptions of Suez. (SZ.)

a.

Dar*a*y*a*v*a*(h)ush khshay*a*thiy*a* v*a*zr*a*k*a* khshay*a*thiy*a* khshay*a*thiyanam khshay*a*thiy*a* d*a*hyunam Vishtasp*a*hya putr*a* H*a*kham*a*nishiy*a*.

b.

B*a*g*a* v*a*zr*a*k*a* Aur*a*m*a*zda hy*a* av*a*m asman*a*m ada hy*a* imam bumim ada hy*a* m*a*rtiy*a*m ada hy*a* shiyatim ada m*a*rtiy*a*hya hy*a* Dar*a*y*a*v*a*(h)um khshay*a*thiy*a*m akun*a*ush hy*a* Dar*a*y*a*v*a*h*a*ush khshay*a*thiy*a*hya khsh*a*tr*a*m frab*a*r*a* ty*a* v*a*zr*a*k*a*m ty*a*.... Ad*a*m Dar*a*y*a*v*a*(h)ush khshay*a*thiy*a* v*a*zr*a*k*a* khshay*a*thiy*a* khshay*a*thiyanam khshay*a*thiy*a* d*a*hyunam p*a*ruvz*a*nanam khshay*a*thiy*a* ahyaya bumiya v*a*zr*a*kaya dur*a*iy apiy Vishtasp*a*hya putr*a* H*a*kham*a*nishiy*a* Thatiy Dar*a*y*a*v*a*(h)ush khshay*a*thiy*a* ad*a*m Pars*a* amiy h*a*da Parsa Mudray*a*m ag*a*rbay*a*m ad*a*m niy*a*shtay*a*m imam yuviyam k*a*(n)t*a*n*a*iy h*a*ca [1]Pirav*a* nam*a* r*a*ut*a* ty*a* Mudray*a*iy d*a*n*a*uv*a*tiy abiy d*a*ray*a* ty*a* h*a*ca Parsa aitiy p*a*sav*a* iy*a*m yuviya (akaniy) av*a*(da) y*a*tha ad*a*m niy*a*shtay*a*m ut......ay*a*ta h*a*ca...ya mam yuviyam abiy pa......ta y*a*tha ma .....

---

[1] Pirav*a* nam*a* r*a*ut*a*, 68.

V.

Inscription of London.

Ad*a*m Dar*ayava*(h)ush khshay*ȧ*thıy*a*.

Inscriptions of Persepolis.

H.

ABOVE THE WALL SURROUNDING THE PALACE OF PERSEPOLIS.

Auramazda vazraka hya mathishta baganam hauv Darayava(h)um khshayathiyam adada haushaiy khshatram frabara vashna Auramazdaha Darayava(h)ush khshayathiya Thatiy Darayava(h)ush khshayathiya iyam dahyaush Parsa tyam mana Auramazdâ frabara hya naiba ([h]uvaspa) (h)umartiya vashna Auramazdaha manaca Darayavahaush khshayathiyahya haca aniyana naiy tarsatiy Thatiy Darayava(h)ush khshayathiya mana Auramazda upastam baratuv hada vithibish bagaibish uta imam dahyaum Auramazda patuv haca hainaya haca dushiyara haca drauga aniya imam dahyaum ma.. ajamiya ma haina ma dushiyaram ma drauga aita adam yan - - m jadiyamiy Auramazdam hada [1]vithibish bagaibish aitamaiy Auramazda dadatuv hada vithibish bagaibish.

I.

ANOTHER INSCRIPTION ABOVE THE WALL.

Adam Darayava(h)ush khshayathiya vazraka khshayathiya khshayathiyanam khshayathiya dahyunam tyaisham parunam Vishtaspahya putra Hakhamanishiya Thatiy Darayava(h)ush khshayathiya vashna Auramazdaha ima dahyava tya adam adarshaiy hada ana Parsa kara tya hacama atarsa(n) mana bajim abara(n) (H)uvaja Mada Babirush Arabaya Athura Mudraya Armina Katapatuka Sparda Yauna tyaiy (h)ushkahya uta tyaiy darayahya uta dahyava tya parauvaiy Asagarta Parthava Zara(n)ka Haraiva Bakhtrish Sugda (H)uvarazamiya Thatagush Harauvatish Hi(n)dush Ga(n)dara Saka Maka Thatiy Darayava(h)ush khshayathiya yadiy avatha maniyahy

---

[1] vithibish bagaibish, 86, c.

[1] h*a*ca aniy*a*na ma t*a*rs*a*m im*a*m Pars*a*m kar*a*m padiy y*a*diy kar*a* Pars*a* pat*a* ah*a*tiy hya duv*a*isht*a*m shiyatish akhsh*a*ta h*a*uvciy Aura nir*a*satiy abiy imam vith*a*m.

B.

OVER THE PILLARS IN THE PALACE.

Dar*a*y*a*v*a*(h)ush khshay*a*thiy*a* v*a*zr*a*k*a* khshay*a*thiy*a* khshay*a*thiyanam khshay*a*thiy*a* d*a*hyunam Vishtap*a*hya putr*a* . Hakham*a*nishiy*a* hy*a* im*a*m t*a*c*a*r*a*m akun*a*ush.

---

[1] h*a*ca aniy*a*na ma t*a*rs*a*m, 77, A; 95, B.

Inscriptions of Naqshi Rustam. (NR)

a.

Baga vazraka Auramazda hya imam bumim ada hya avam asmanam ada hya martiyam ada hya shiyatim ada martiyahya hya Darayava(h)um khshayathiyam akunaush aivam paruvnam khshayathiyam aivam paruvnam framataram Adam Darayava(h)ush khshayathiya vazraka khshayathiya khshayathiyanam khshayathiya dahyunam vispazananam khshayathiya ahyaya bumiya vazakaya duraiy apiy Vishtaspahya putra Hakhamanishiya Parsa Parsahya putra Ariya Ariya citra Thatiy Darayava(h)ush khshayathiya vashna Auramazdaha ima dahyava tya adam agarbayam [1]apataram haca Parsa [2]adamsham patiyakhshaiy mana bajim abara(n)t(a) tyasham hacama athahy ava akunava(n) datam tya mana aita adari Mada (H)uvaja Parthava Haraiva Bakhtrish Suguda (H)uvarazamish Zara(n)ka Harauvatish Thatagush Ga(n)dara Hi(n)dush Saka Humavarka Saka Tigrakhauda Babirush Athura Arabaya Mudraya Armina Katapatuka Sparda [3]Yauna Saka tyaiy taradaraya Skudra Yauna Takabara Putiya Kushiya Maciya Karka Thatiy Darayava(h)ush khshayathiya Auramazda yatha avaina imam bumim yu - - - - pasavadim mana frabara mam khshayathiyam akunaush adam khshayathiya amiy vashna Auramazdaha adamshim gathva niyashadayam [4]tyasham adam athaham ava akunava(n)ta yatha mam kama aha yadiyadiy tya [5]ciya(n)karam ava dahyava tya Darayava(h)ush khshayathiya adaraya patikaram didiy tyaiy mana gathum bara(n)tiy yatha [6]khshnasahadish adataiy azda bavatiy Parsahya martiyahya duray arshtish paragmata adataiy azda bavatiy Parsa martiya

---

[1] apataram haca Parsa, 78. [2] adamsham patiyakhshaiy, 83, B. [3] Yauna, 86, B, Note 1. [4] tyasham - akunava(n)ta, 60, A. [5] ciya(n)karam ava dahyava, 86. [6] khshnasahadish, 83, B.

duray haca Parsa hamaram patiyajata Thatiy Darayava(h)ush khshayathiya aita tya kartam ava visam vashna Auramazdaha akunavam Auramazdamaiy upastam abara yata kartam akunavam mam Auramazda patuv haca sar - - - utamaiy vitham uta imam dahyaum [1]aita adam Auramazdam jadiyamiy aitamaiy Auramazda dadatuv Martiya hya Auramazdaha framana hauvtaiy gasta ma thadaya pathim tyam rastam ma avarada ma starava.

b.

Baga vazraka Auramazda hya ada - - - - - f - - - - - m tya va - - - - - ada shiyatim martiyahya - - - - - u - - - a aruvastam upariy Darayava(h)um khshayathiyam - - - iyasaya Thatiy Darayava(h)ush khshayathiya vashna Auramazdaha - - - - - kar - - - - - - iya tya - - - - a - - - - tam - - - - - - - ya - - - daush - - - - - - - athiy n - - - - - - - sh - - - - - uva - - - ya - - - - - yim karimish - - - - - vasim tya - - - - - - - - - - - - r - - - - - - iya - - - im - - - - - riyish - - - - - - ava - - m - - - - - - m m - - - - - m dar - - - - - - ush - - - a - - - - - - uvish a - - - - - - - - - miy - - - - - ya - - - - astiy darshama da - - - - ya - - - - - au - - - - - - - iyahya darshama - - - - - - -

c.

Gaubaruva Patishuvarish Darayavahaush khshayathiyahya sharastibara.

d.

Aspacana Darayavahaush khshayathiyahya isuvam dasyama.

e.

Iyam Maciya.

---

[1] aita adam Auramazdam jadiyamiy, 64.

VI.

THE INSCRIPTIONS OF XERXES.

The Inscriptions of Persepolis.

D.

UPON EACH ONE OF THE FOUR PILLARS OF THE ENTRANCES TO THE PALACE OF XERXES.

Baga vazraka Auramazda hya imam bumim ada hya martiyam ada hya shiyatim ada martiyahya hya Khshayarsham khshayathiyam akunaush aivam parunam framataram Adam Khshayarsha khshayathiya vazraka khshayathiya khshayathiyanam khshayathiya dahyunam paruvzananam khshayathiya ahyaya bumiya vazrakaya duraiy apiy Darayavahaush khshayathiyahya putra Hakhamanishiya Thatiy Khshayarsha khshayathiya vazraka vashna Auramazdaha imam duvarthim visadahyum adam akunavam vasiy aniyashciy naibam kartam [1]ana Parsa tya adam akunavam utamaiy tya pita akunaush tyapatiy kartam vainataiy naibam ava visam vashna Auramazdaha akuma Thatiy Khshayarsha khshayathiya mam Auramazda patuv utamaiy khshatram uta tya mana kartam uta tyamaiy pitra kartam avashciy Auramazda patuv.

G.

UPON THE PILLARS ON THE WESTERN SIDE OF THE PALACE.

Khshayarsha khshayathiya vazraka khshayathiya khshayathiyanam Darayavahaush khshayathiyahya putra Hakhamanishiya.

---

[1] ana Parsa, 73.

Ea.

UPON THE WALL BY THE STEPS OF THE PALACE.

Baga vazraka Auramazda hya imam bumim ada hya avam asmanam ada hya martiyam ada hya shiyatim ada martiyahya hya Khshayarsham khshayathiyam akunaush aivam parunam khshayathiyam aivam parunam framataram Adam Khshayarsha khshayathiya vazraka khshayathiya khshayathiyanam khshayathiya dahyunam paruvzananam khshayathiya ahiyaya bumiya vazrakaya duraiy apiy Darayavahaush khshayathiyahya putra Hakhamanishiya Thatiy Khshayarsha khshayathiya vazraka vashna Auramazdaha ima hadish adam akunavam mam Auramazda patuv hada bagaibish utamaiy khshatram uta tyamaiy kartam.

Eb.

Baga vazraka Auramazda hya imam bumim ada hya avam asmanam ada hya martiyam ada hya shiyatim ada martiyahya hya Khshayarsham khshayathiyam akunaush aivam parunam khshayathiyam aivam parunam framataram Adam Khshayarsha khshayathiya vazraka khshayathiya khshayathiyanam khshayathiya dahyunam paruvzananam khshayathiya ahiyaya bumiya vazrakaya duraiy apiy Darayavahaush khshayathiyahya putra Hakhamanishiya Thatiy Khshayarsha khshayathiya vazraka vashna Auramazdaha ima hadish adam akunavam mam Auramazda patuv hada bagaibish utamaiy khshatram uta tyamaiy kartam.

Ca.

UPON THE HIGHEST PILLAR NEAR THE SOUTHERN STEPS.

Baga vazraka Auramazda hya imam bumim ada hya avam asmanam ada hya martiyam ada shiyatim ada martiyahya hya Khshayarsham khshayathiyam.

akunaush aivam parunam khshayathiyam aivam parunam framataram Adam Khshayarsha khshayathiya vazraka khshayathiya khshayathiyanam khshayathiya dahyunam [1]paruv zananam khshayathiya ahyaya bumiya vazrakaya duraiy apiy Darayavahaush khshayathiyahya putra Hakhamanishiya Thatiy Khshayarsha khshayathiya vazraka vashna Aurahya Mazdaha ima hadish Darayava(h)ush khshayathiya akunaush hya mana pita mam Auramazda patuv hada bagaibish uta tyamaiy kartam uta tyamaiy pitra Darayavahaush khshayathiyahya kartam avashciy Auramazda patuv hada bagaibish.

Cb.

Baga vazraka Auramazda hya imam bumim ada hya avam asmanam ada hya martiyam ada hya shiyatim ada martiyahya hya Khshayarsham khshayathiyam akunaush aivam parunam khshayathiyam aivam parunam framataram Adam Khshayarsha khshayathiya vazraka khshayathiya khshayathiyanam khshayathiya dahyunam [1]paruv zananam khshayathiya ahyaya bumiya vazrakaya duraiy apiy Darayavahaush khshayathiyahya putra Hakhamanishiya Thatiy Khshayarsha khshayathiya vazraka vashna Aurahya Mazdaha ima hadish Darayava(h)ush khshayathiya akunaush hya mana pita mam Auramazda patuv hada bagaibish uta tyamaiy kartam uta tyamaiy pitra Darayavahaush khshayathiyahya kartam avashciy Auramazda patuv hada bagaibish.

A.

UPON THE STEPS OF THE PALACE.

Baga vazraka Auramazda hya imam bumim ada avam asmanam ada hya martiyam ada hya shiyatim ada martiyahya hya Khshayarsham khshayathiyam

---

[1] paruv zananam, 104, Note.

akun*a*ush aiv*a*m p*a*runam khshay*a*thiy*a*m aiv*a*m p*a*runam fr*a*matar*a*m Ad*a*m Khsh*a*yarsha khshay*a*thiy*a* v*a*zr*a*k*a* khshay*a*thiy*a* khshay*a*thiyanam khshay*a*thiy*a* d*a*hyunam p*a*ruvz*a*nanam khshay*a*thiy*a* ahiyaya bumiya v*a*zr*a*kaya dur*a*iy apiy Dar*a*y*a*v*a*h*a*ush khshay*a*thiy*a*hya putr*a* Hakham*a*nishiy*a* Thatiy Khsh*a*yarsha khshay*a*thiy*a* v*a*zr*a*k*a* ty*a* m*a*na k*a*rt*a*m ida uta ty*a*m*a*iy ap*a*t*a*r*a*m k*a*rt*a*m av*a* vis*a*m v*a*shna Aur*a*m*a*zdah*a* akun*a*v*a*m mam Aur*a*m*a*zda patuv h*a*da b*a*g*a*ibish utam*a*iy khsh*a*tr*a*m uta ty*a*m*a*iy k*a*rt*a*m.

Inscription of Alvend.

F.

Baga vazraka Auramazda hya mathishta baganam hya imam bumim ada hya avam asmanam ada hya martiyam ada hya shiyatim ada martiyahya hya Khshayarsham khshayathiyam akunaush aivam parunam khshayathiyam aivam parunam framataram Adam Khshayarsha khshayathiya vazraka khshayathiya khshayathiyanam khshayathiya dahyunam paruzananam khshayathiya ahiyaya bumiya vazrakaya duraiy apiy Darayavahaush khshayathiya hya putra Hakhamanishiya.

Inscription of Van.

K.

Baga vazraka Auramazda hya mathista baganam hya imam bumim ada hya avam asmanam ada hya martiyam ada hya shiyatim ada martiyahya hya Khshayarsham khshayathiyam akunaush aivam parunam khshayathiyam aivam parunam framataram Adam Khshayarsha khshayathiya vazraka khshayathiya khshayathiyanam khshayathiya dahyunam [1]paruv zananam khshayathiya ahyaya bumiya vazrakaya duraiy apiy Darayavahaush khshayathiyahya putra Hakhamanishiya Thatiy Khshayarsha khshayathiya Darayava(h)ush khshayathiya hya mana pita hauv vashna Auramazdaha vasiy tya naibam akunaush uta ima stanam hauv niyashtaya ka(n)tanaiy yanaiy dipim naiy nipishtam akunaush pasava adam niyashtayam imam dipim nipishtanaiy (Mam Auramazda patuv hada bagaibish utamaiy khshatram uta tyamaiy kartam).

Qa.

UPON THE VASE OF COUNT CAYLUS.

Khshayarsha khshayathiya vazraka.

---

[1] paruv zananam, 104, Note.

VII.

INSCRIPTIONS OF PERSIAN KINGS

AFTER

XERXES.

ARTAXERXES I.

Inscription at Venice.

Qb.

UPON THE VASE IN THE TREASURY OF ST. MARKS.

Ard*a*khc*a*shc*a* khshay*a*thiy*a* v*a*zr*a*k*a*.

DARIUS II.

Inscriptions of Persepolis.

L.

ABOVE THE POSTS OF THE WINDOWS IN THE PALACE OF DARIUS HYSTASPES.

Ard*a*stan*a* ath*a*(n)g*a*in*a* Dar*ayava*h*a*ush khshay*a*-iy*a*hya vithiya k*a*rt*a*.

ARTAXERXES MNEMON.*

Inscriptions of Susa. (S.)

a.

UPON THE BASE OF THE PILLARS OF A SMALL ROW OF COLUMNS.

Ad*a*m Art*a*khsh*a*tra khshay*a*thiy*a* v*a*zr*a*k*a* khshay*a*thiy*a* khshay*a*thiyanam [1]Dar*a*y*a*v*a*(h)ush*a*hya khshay*a*thiy*a*hya putr*a*.

b.

UPON THE BASE OF THE PILLARS IN THE LARGE ROW OF COLUMNS.

Thatiy Atr*a*khsh*a*tra khshay*a*thiy*a* v*a*zr*a*k*a* khshay*a*thiy*a* khshay*a*thiyanam khshay*a*thiy*a* d*a*hyunam khshay*a*thiy*a* ahyaya bumiya Dar*a*y*a*v*a*(h)ush*a*hya

---

[1] Dar*a*y*a*v*a*(h)ush*a*hya, 85, A; 24.

* An ingenious attempt to make syntax out of the loose construction shown in these inscriptions of Artaxerxes Mnemon and Artaxerxes Ochus, is the following:

Dar*a*y*a*v*a*(h)ush Vishtasp*a*hya nam*a* putr*a* "D. sohn eines mit namen V" Das folgende jedoch Vishtasp*a*hya Arsham*a* nam*a* putr*a* zeigt wie die vorhergehende genealogische aufzählung eine anakoluthe verbindung zweier nominative, von denen der eine zum andern im genetivverhältnis steht. So merkwürdig das anakoluth in P) ist, so wird es doch durch ein analogon gestützt: es entspricht genau der construction Sz b) h*a*ca Pirav*a* nam*a* r*a*ut*a*. In beiden fällen ist statt eines obliquen casus der nominativ gesetzt in folge einer art verkürzung einer bei den alten Persern häufigen pleonastischen ausdruckweise: wie h*a*ca—Pirav*a* nam*a* r*a*ut*a* vollständig lauten müsste h*a*ca r*a*uta—Pirav*a* nam*a* r*a*ut*a*—h*a*ca ada, ebenso an unserer stelle m*a*rtiy*a*hya—Arsham*a* nam*a* m*a*rtiy*a*—av*a*hya putr*a*. Eine solche lose anreihung zweier in abhängigkeitsverhältnis zu denkender glieder ist etwas ganz gewöhnliches, z. b. Nisaya nam*a* d*a*hy*a*ush—av*a*d*a*shim avaj*a*n*a*m (Bh I), (V*a*umis*a*) nam*a* Pars*a* b*a*(n)d*a*k*a* av*a*m ad*a*m fr*a*ish*a*y*a*m (II). Diese constructionen unterscheiden sich von der unsrigen nur dadurch, dass die wiederaufnahme des abhängigen satzgliedes durch eine oblique pronominalform sowohl Sz b) wie an unserer stelle nicht stattgefunden hat. Es ist eine jedermann verständliche vereinfachung jener umständlichen und schwerfällinen ausdrucksweise.

In P) ist auch das wort nam*a*, welches ursprünglich die bedingung der anakoluthen construction ist, als entbehrlich über bord geworfen: Art*a*khsh*a*tra Dar*a*y*a*v*a*(h)ush khshay*a*thiy*a* putr*a* ist also die

khshay*a*thiy*a*hya· putr*a* Dar*a*y*a*v*a*(h)ush*a*hya Art*a*-khsh*a*trahya khshay*a*thiy*a*hya putr*a* Art*a*khsh*a*trahya Khsh*a*yarsh*a*hya khshay*a*thiy*a*hya putr*a* Khsh*a*yar-sh*a*hya Dar*a*y*a*v*a*(h)ush*a*hya khshay*a*thiy*a*hya putr*a* Dar*a*y*a*v*a*(h)ush*a*hya Vishtashp*a*hya putr*a* H*a*khama-nishiy*a* [1]Im*a*m ap*a*dan*a* Dar*a*y*a*v*a*(h)ush ap*a*nyak*a*m*a* [2]akun*a*sh abiy*a*p*a*r*a*....pa Art*a*khsh*a*tra nyak*a*m*a*... An*a*h*a*t*a* uta Mithr*a* v*a*shna Aur*a*m*a*zdah*a* ap*a*dana ad*a*m akun*a*v*a*m Aur*a*m*a*zda An*a*h*a*t*a* uta Mithr*a* mam patuv ...

---

weiterentwicklung und vereinfachung des älteren typus Art*a*khsh*a*-tra khshay*a*thiy*a*hya — Dar*a*y*a*v*a*(h)ush nam*a* khshay*a*thiy*a* — av*a*hya putr*a* "A sohn eines königs — es ist ein könig Darius mit namen — dessen sohn."

Noch eine andere eigenheit enthält die inschrift, nämlich den genetiv Vishtap*a*hya, wo wir einen nominativ erwarten. Dieselbe construction findet sich durchgängig in S. Die wiederholung des namens im genetiv statt im nominativ dient zu emphatischer hervorhebung und ist eine assimilatorische anlehnung an den vorhergehenden genetiv, während das subjekt aus dem genetiv zu ergänzen ist· Dar*a*y*a*v*a*(h)ush*a*hya khshay*a*thiy*a*hya putr*a*, Dar*a*v*a*y*a*(h)ush*a*hya (hy*a*) Art*a*khsh*a*tr*a*hya putr*a* "des Darius sohn, (jenes) Darius, (der) des Artaxerxes sohn (war), jenes Artaxerxes, der des Xerxes sohn war u s. w —

[1] Im*a*m ap*a*dad*a*, 85, B. [2]akun*a*sh, 42.

ARTAXERXES OCHUS.

Inscription of Persepolis.

P.

UPON THE STEPS OF THE PALACE OF DARIUS HYSTASPES AND ARTAXERXES OCHUS.

Baga vazraka Auramazda hya imam bumam ada hya avam asmanam ada hya martiyam ada hya shayatam ada martihya hya mam Artakhshatra khshayathiya akunaush aivam paruvnam khshayathiyam aivam paruvnam framataram Thatiy Artakhshatra khshayathiya vazraka khshayathiya khshayathiyanam khshayathiya dahyunam khshayathiya ahyaya bumiya Adam Artakhshatra khshayathiya putra Artakhshatra Darayava(h)ush khshayathiya putra Artakhshatra khshayathiya putra Artakhshatra Khshayarsha khshayathiya putra Khshayarsha Darayava(h)ush V(i)shtaspahya nama putra V(i)shtaspahya Arshama nama putra Hakhamanishiya Thatiy Artakhshatra khshayathiya imam usatashanam [2]atha(n)ganam mam upa mam karta Thatiy Artakhshatra khshayathiya mam Auramazda uta M(i)thra baga patuv uta imam dahyum uta [3]tya mam karta.

---

[1] Darayava(h)ush, 85, c. [2] atha(n)ganam, 85, d; 86, d. [3] tya mam karta, 85, e and f.

ARSACES.

R.

INSCRIPTION UPON THE SEAL OF GROTEFEND.

Arsh*a*k*a* nam*a* Athiyad*a*ush*a*n*a*hya putr*a*.

THE

CUNEIFORM TEXT*

OF THE

INSCRIPTIONS OF DARIUS

AT

ALVEND, SUEZ, PERSEPOLIS

AND

NAQSHI RUSTAM.

---

* The inscriptions are taken from a pen sketch made by the author.

For the Cuneiform text of the Behistan the student is referred to the great work of Rawlinson in Vol. X of the Royal Asiatic Society of Great Britain and Ireland. The author is under much obligation to Dr Kossowicz, Professor of Sanskrit in the Imperial University of St. Petersburg.

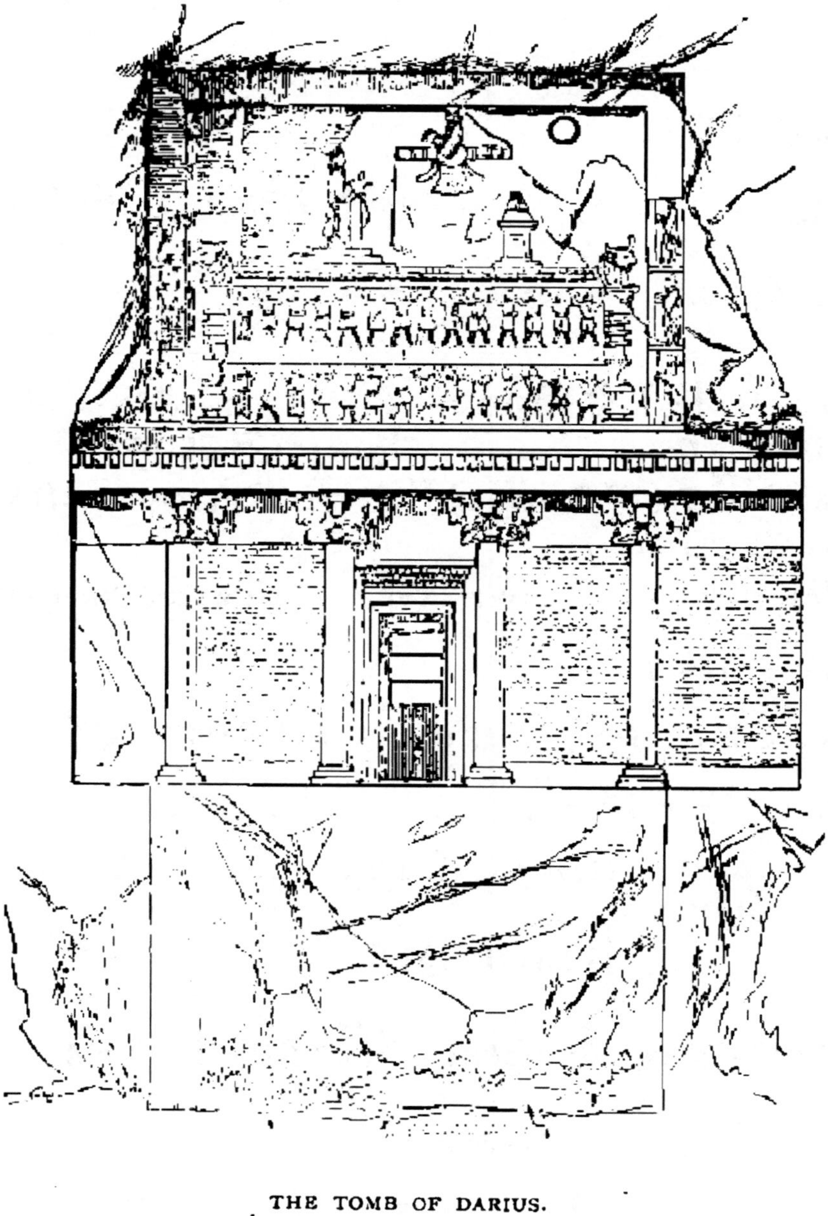

THE TOMB OF DARIUS.

THE CUNEIFORM ALPHABET.

- GUTTURAL 𐎠 Ā
- PALATAL 𐎡 I
- LABIAL 𐎢 U

SONANT SIBILANT 𐏀 Z

- GUTTURAL 𐎣 K (𐎤 BEFORE U) 𐎧 KH 𐎥 G (𐎦 BEFORE U)
- PALATAL 𐎨 C 𐎪 J (𐎩 BEFORE U)
- DENTAL 𐎫 T (𐎬 BEFORE U) 𐎰 TH 𐎭 D (𐎯 BEFORE U, 𐎮 BEFORE I)
- 𐎴 N (𐎵 BEFORE U)
- LABIAL 𐎱 P 𐎳 F 𐎲 B 𐎶 M (𐎸 BEFORE U, 𐎷 BEFORE I)

- PALATAL 𐎹 Y.
- LINGUAL 𐎼 R (𐎽 BEFORE U)
- LABIAL 𐎺 V (𐎻 BEFORE I)

ASPIRATION 𐏃

SIBILANTS:
- LINGUAL 𐏁 SH
- DENTAL 𐎿 S

𐏋 = KHSHĀYATHIYA, 𐏏 = BUMI, 𐏌 = DAH, 𐏂 = TRA.

NUMERALS

𐏑 1 𐏒𐏑 3 𐏓 10 𐏓𐏒 12 𐏔 20

𐏒 2 𐏒𐏒 4 𐏓𐏑 11 𐏓𐏒𐏑 13 𐏔𐏑 21

ETC. ETC.

(O)

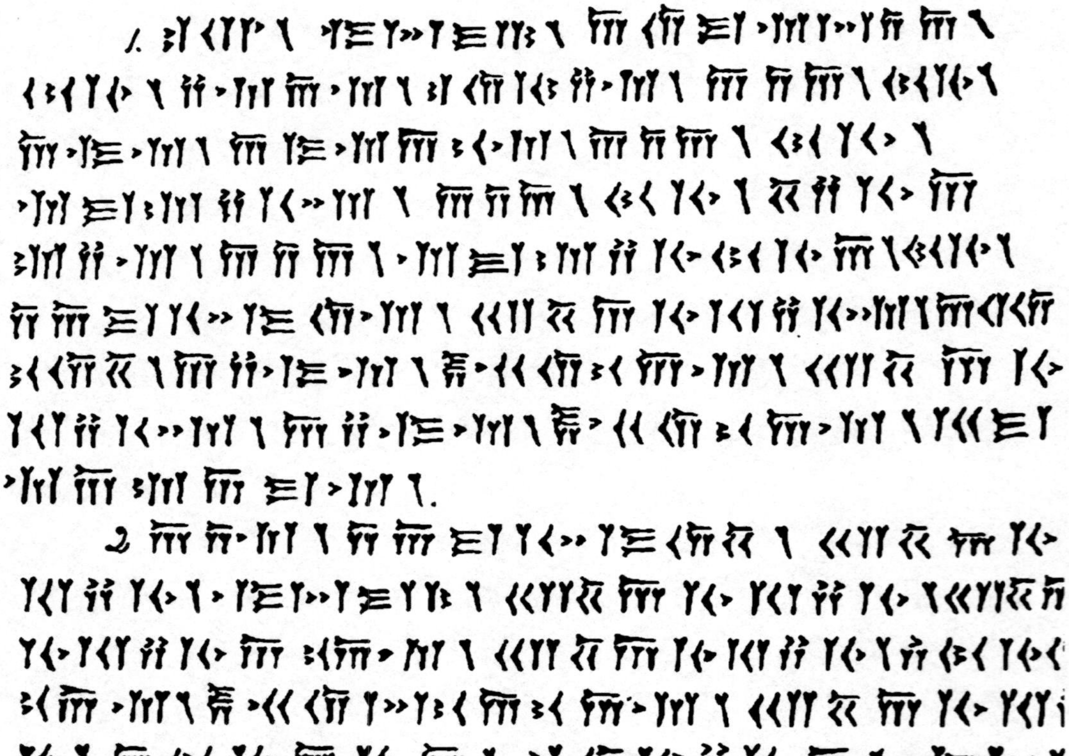

(SZ)

a

[illegible]

b

1. [illegible]

2. [illegible]

3. [illegible]

[illegible]

(London)

[illegible]

(H)

1. [illegible]

2 [illegible]

3. [illegible]

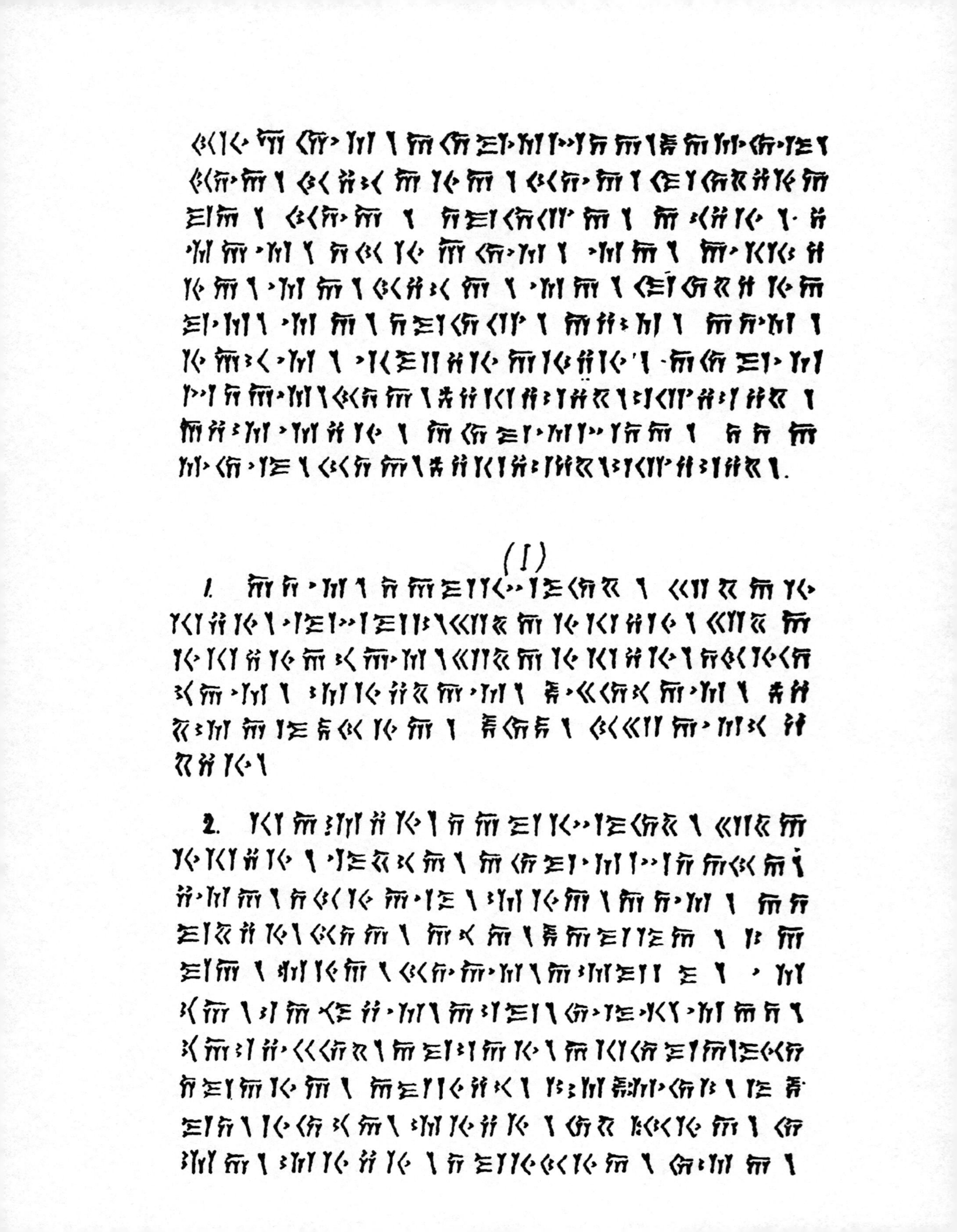

[illegible]
[illegible]
[illegible]
[illegible]
[illegible]
[illegible]
[illegible]
[illegible]
[illegible]
[illegible].

(I)

1. [illegible]
[illegible]
[illegible]
[illegible]
[illegible]
[illegible]

2. [illegible]
[illegible]
[illegible]
[illegible]
[illegible]
[illegible]
[illegible]
[illegible]
[illegible]
[illegible]

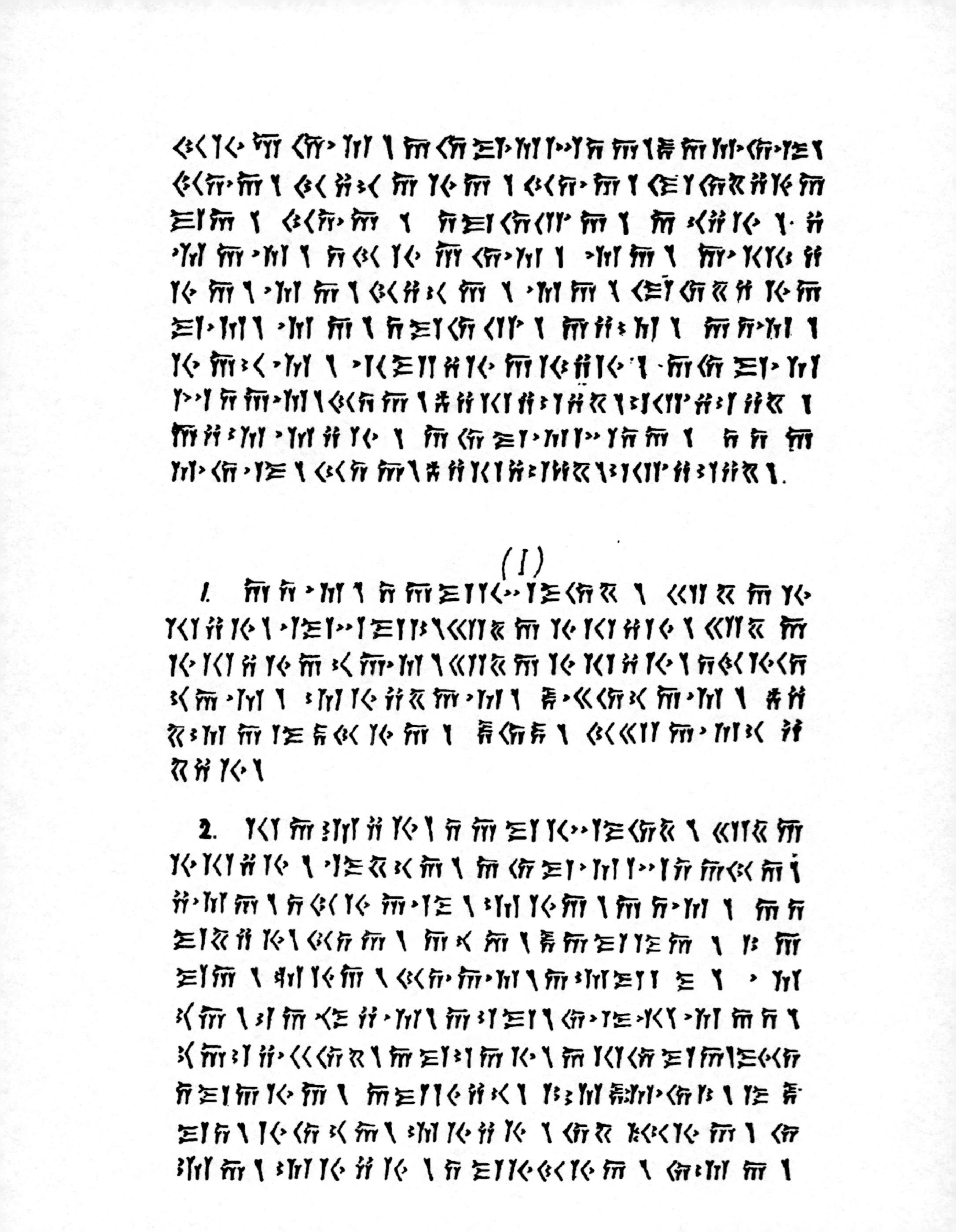

[illegible]
[illegible]
[illegible]
[illegible]
[illegible]
[illegible]
[illegible]
[illegible]
[illegible]
[illegible]

(I)

1. [illegible]
[illegible]
[illegible]
[illegible]
[illegible]
[illegible]

2. [illegible]
[illegible]
[illegible]
[illegible]
[illegible]
[illegible]
[illegible]
[illegible]
[illegible]
[illegible]

[illegible]

3. [illegible]

(B)

[illegible]

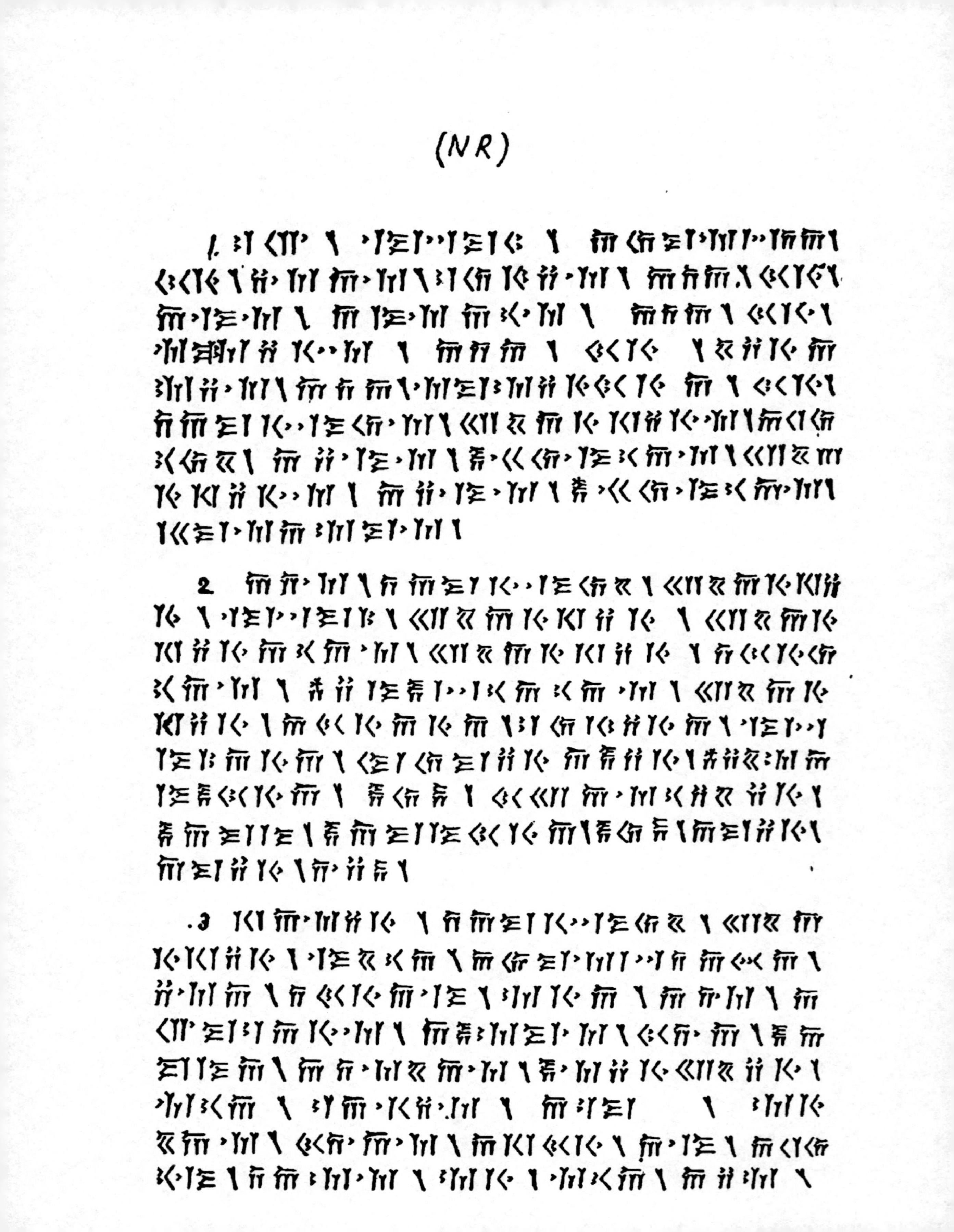

(NR)

1. [illegible]

2. [illegible]

3. [illegible]

4.

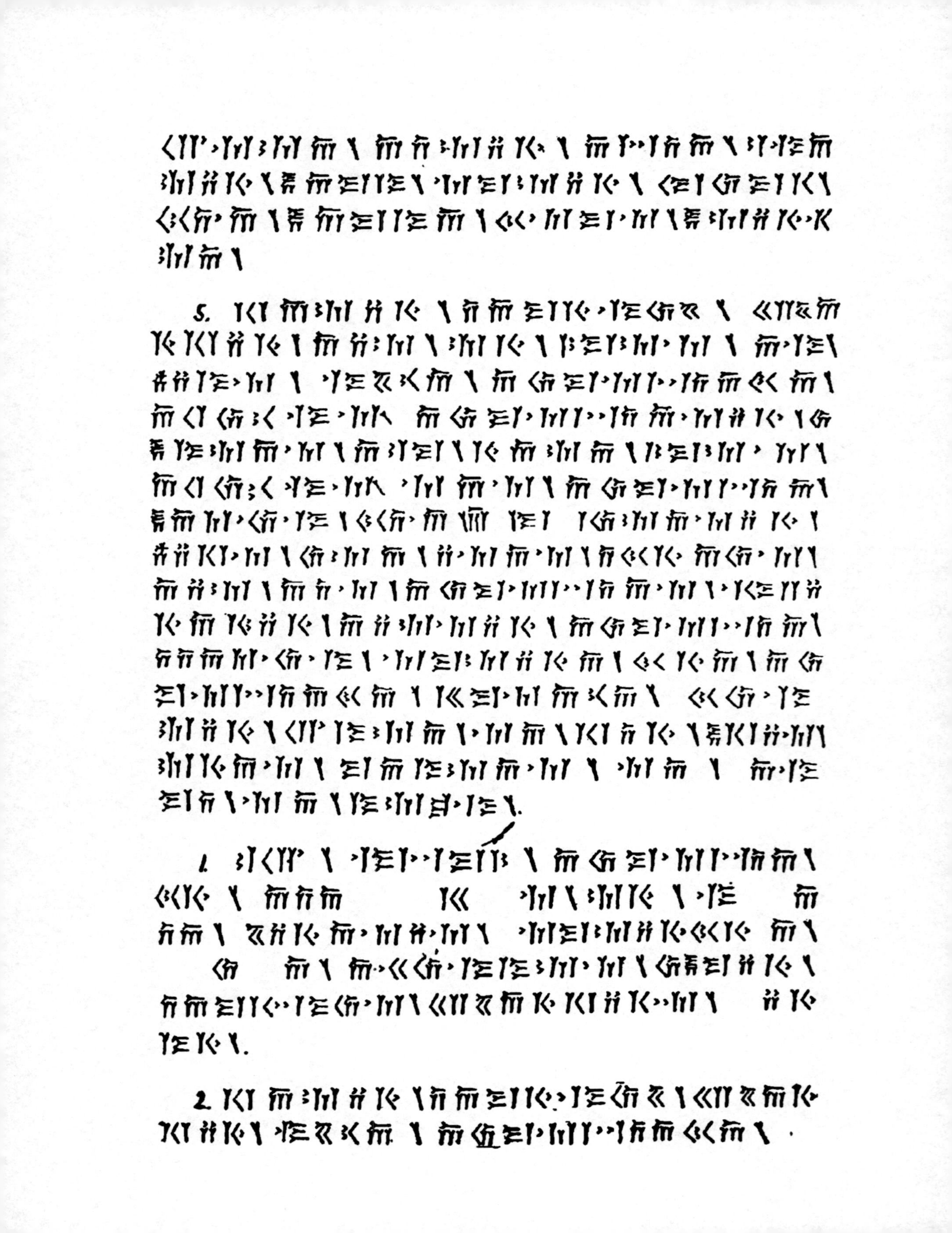

[illegible]

5. [illegible]

1. [illegible]

2. [illegible]

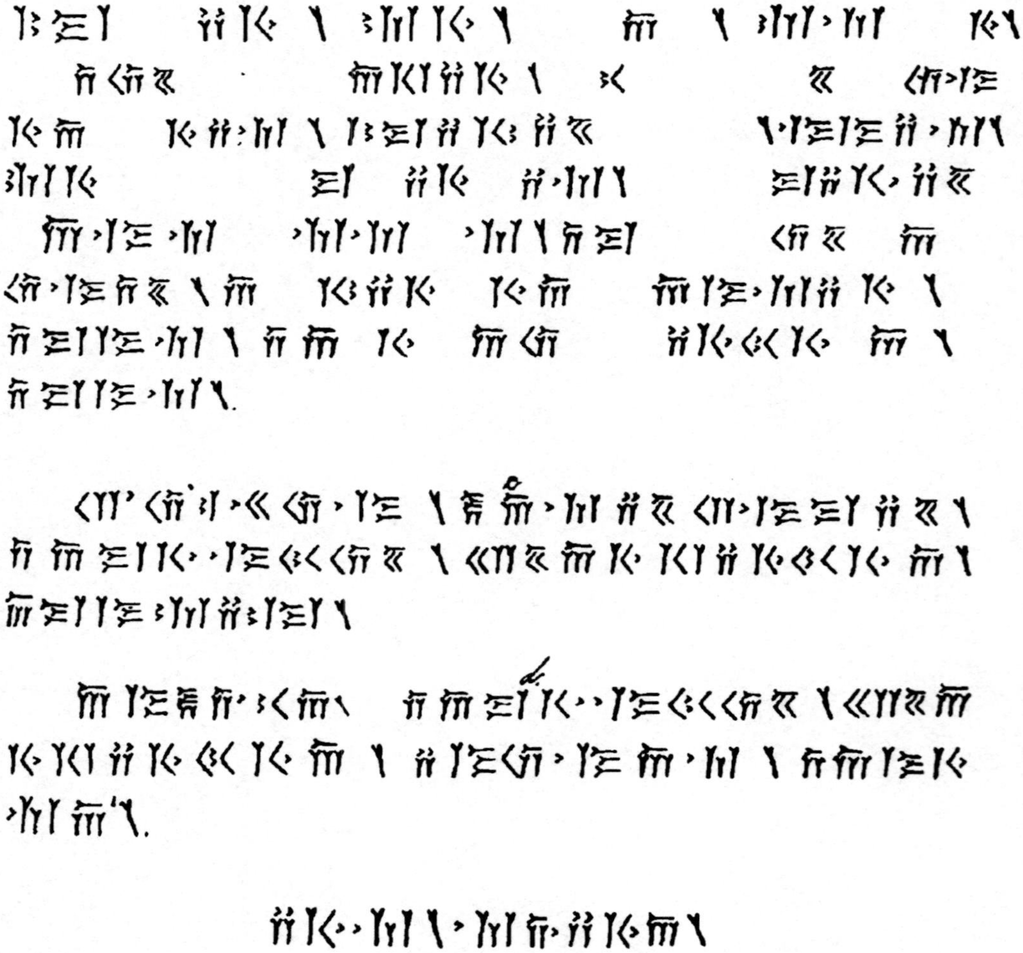

TRANSLATION

OF THE

INSCRIPTIONS.

THE "SEPULCHRAL' INSCRIPTION OF CYRUS. (M.)

(PERSIAN, MEDIAN, ASSYRIAN.)

The oldest inscription of Persia is found on that structure generally believed to be the tomb of Cyrus. At Pasargadæ, in the midst of the plain of Murghab, stands a building of white marble rising to the height of thirty-six feet from the ground. Its base is forty-seven feet long and forty-four feet broad. A figure in bas-relief carved on a pillar, perhaps the portrait of the king himself, strengthens the theory that this structure is the tomb of Cyrus. A narrow doorway leads into an inner chamber, where Arrian says, the body of Cyrus was placed. Under the relief is the cuneiform inscription, the translation of which follows:

TRANSLATION.

I (am) Cyrus, the king, the Achæmenide.

For the sake of comparison the reader is referred to the epitaph of Cyrus quoted by Strabo, (XV, 3.)

THE INSCRIPTION OF DARIUS HYSTASPES AT BEHISTAN.* (BH.)

(PERSIAN, [MEDIAN, ASSYRIAN])

1. I (am) Darius, the great king, the king of kings, the king of Persia, the king of countries, the son of Hystaspes, the grandson Arshama, the Achæmenide.

2. Says Darius the king, my father (is) Hystaspes, the father of Hystaspes (is) Arshama, the father of Arshama (is) Ariyaramna, the father of Ariyaramna (is Caispis), the father of Caispis (is) Achæmenes.

3. Says Darius the king, therefore we are called the Achæmenides: from long ago we have extended† from long ago our family have been kings.

4 Says Darius the king VIII.‡ of my family (there were) who were formerly kings: I am the IX: individually we were (lit. are) kings.

5. Says Darius the king by the grace of Auramazda I am king: Auramazda gave me the kingdom.

6 Says Darius the king these are the countries which came to me: by the grace of Auramazda I became king of them, Persia, Susiana, Babylon, Assyria, Arabia, Egypt, which are by the sea, Sparda, Ionia, Media, Armenia, Cappadocia, Parthia, Drangiana, Area, Chorasmia, Bactriana, Sogdiana, Gandara, Saka, Thatagus, Haravatis, Maka, in all (there are) XXIII countries.

---

*This inscription contains nearly one thousand lines Cf Introduction

†The Persian word AMATA is connected with the Sanskrit root MA *to measure* (Cf Zend MA and Latin ME-TO) The A is doubtless a prefix corresponding to the Sanskrit A (hither) AMATA would mean *measured hither* or *to the present time*, i e, reaching to the present It is possible to emphasize the idea of the root MA (measure)· hence the word might signify *measured, tested, tried*

‡The numerals are represented by horizontal wedges for units and oblique for the tens Cf. Cuneiform alphabet

7. Says Darius the king these (are) the countries which came to me: by the grace of Auramazda they became subject to me: they bore tribute to me: what was commanded to them by me this was done night and (lit. or) day.

8. Says Darius the king within these countries what man was a friend* him well supported I supported: who was an enemy him well punished I punished; by the grace of Auramazda these countries followed my law: as it was commanded by me to them, so it was done.

9. Says Darius the king Auramazda gave me the kingdom: Auramazda bore me aid until this kingdom was established: by the grace of Auramazda I hold this kingdom.

10 Says Darius the king this (is) what (was) done by me after that I became king; Cambyses by name, the son of Cyrus (was) of our family: he before was king here: of this Cambyses there was a brother Bardiya (i. e., Smerdis) by name possessing a common mother and the same father with Cambyses; afterwards Cambyses slew that Bardiya: when Cambyses slew Bardiya there was not knowledge† (on the part) of the state that Bardiya was slain: afterwards Cambyses went to Egypt: when Cambyses went to Egypt, after that the state became hostile, after that there was deceit to a great extent in the provinces, both Persia and Media and other provinces.

11. Says Darius the king afterwards there was one man, a Magian, Gaumata by name; he rose up from Paishiyauvada; there (is) a mountain Arakadris, by

---

* The Persian word is of doubtful interpretation. It looks like the NOMEN AGENTIS of GAM *to go*, *a goer hither* or *a comer* The translation *friend* is a conventional one.

† AZDA, a doubtful word I connect it with the root DA *to know* which occurs in the compound AURAMAZDA.

name; from there on the 14th day* of the month Viyakhna then it was when he rose up: he then deceived the state; I am Bardiya the son of Cyrus brother of Cambyses: afterwards the whole state became estranged from Cambyses (and) went over to him, both Persia and Media and the other provinces: he seized the kingdom; on the 9th day of the month Garmapada then it was he thus seized the kingdom; afterward Cambyses died by a self-imposed death †

12. Says Darius the king this kingdom which Gaumata the Magian took from Cambyses, this kingdom from long ago was (the possession) of our family: afterwards Gaumata the Magian took from Cambyses both Persia and Media and the other provinces; he acted in accordance with? his own power? he became king.

13. Says Darius the king there was not a man neither a Persian nor Median nor any one of our family who could make Gaumata the Magian deprived of the kingdom; the state feared him vehemently (or because of his violence), he would smite the state utterly which knew the former Bardiya; for this reason he would smite the state that it might not know me ‡ that I am not Bardiya the son of Cyrus, any one did not dare to say anything against Gaumata the Magian until I came; afterwards I asked Auramazda for help; Auramazda bore me aid; on the 10th day of the month Bagayadis then it was I thus with (my) faithful? men slew that Gaumata the Magian and

*Lit. with fourteen days; a use of the instrumental which denotes the association of time with an event. This idiom is employed in all like temporal expressions Cf Grammar, 72

† The word UVAMARSHIYUSH can be divided into UVA *self* (Cf Skt *sva* Lat. SE) and MARSHIYUSH *die* (Cf. Skt MAR Lat MORIOR) The meaning also corresponds to the statement in Herodotus III 64-65, that Cambyses died from a wound inflicted by his sword as he was leaping from his horse

‡ Note the direct form of expression.

what men were his foremost allies; there (is) a stronghold Sikayauvatis by name;* there is a province in Media Visaya by name; here I smote him; I took the kingdom from him; by the grace of Auramazda I became king: Auramazda gave me the kingdom.

14. Says Darius the king—the kingdom which was taken away from our family, this I put in (its) place; I established it on (its) foundation; as (it was) formerly so I made it; the sanctuaries? which Gaumata the Magian destroyed I restored. The commerce? of the state and the cattle and the dwelling places, and (I did this) in accordance with† the clans, which Gaumata the Magian took from them, (I restored); I established the state on (its) foundation both Persia and Media and the other provinces; as (it was) formerly so I brought back what (had been) taken away; by the grace of Auramazda this I did; I labored that our clan I might establish in (its) place; as (it was) formerly, so (I made it); I labored by the grace of Auramazda that Gaumata the Magian might not take away our race.

15. Says Darius the king this (is) what I did, after that I became king.

16. Says Darius the king when I slew Gaumata the Magian afterwards there (was) one man Atrina by name the son of Upadara(n)ma; he rose up in Uvaja; (i. e., Susiana); thus he said to the state; I am king in Uvaja; afterwards the people of Uvaja became rebellious (and) went over to that Atrina; he became king in Uvaja; also there (was) one man a Babylonian Naditabira by name the son of Ain....; he rose up in Babylon; thus he deceived the state; I am Na-

* NAM*a* is not the accusative of specification, but is attracted into the case, and even the gender of the subject Lit there is a stronghold (its) name (is) Sikayauvatis Cf. Grammar, 61, A. Note 2, but cf Bartholomæ, Arische Forsch I, 58

† Cf Grammar, 70, A

bukudracara the son of Nabunita; afterwards the whole of the Babylonian state went over to that Naditabira; Babylon became rebellious; the kingdom in Babylon he seized.

17. Says Darius the king afterwards I sent forth (my army) to Uvaja; this Atrina was led to me bound; I slew him.

18. Says Darius the king afterwards I went to Babylon against that Naditabira who called himself Nabukudracara; the army of Naditabira held the Tigris; there he halted and was on shipboard; afterwards I destroyed the army...... one (army) I made submissive, of the other...... I led; Auramazda bore me aid; by the grace of Auramazda we crossed the Tigris; here the army of Naditabira I slew utterly; on the 27th day of the month Atriyadiya then it was we thus engaged in battle.

19. Says Darius the king afterwards I went to Babylon; when to Babylon......................; there (is) a town Zazana by name along the Euphrates; there this Naditabira who called himself Nabukudracara went with his army against me to engage in battle; afterwards we engaged in battle; Auramazda bore me aid; by the grace of Auramazda the army of Naditabira I slew utterly.................... the water bore it away; on the 2nd day of the month Anamaka then it was we thus engaged in battle.

II.

1. Says Darius the king afterwards Naditabira with (his) faithful ? horsemen went to Babylon; afterwards I went to Babylon; by the grace of Auramazda I both seized Babylon and seized that Naditabira; afterwards I slew that Naditabira at Babylon.

2. Says Darius the king while I was in Babylon these (are) the provinces which became estranged from me, Persia, Uvaja, Media, Assyria, Armenia, Parthia, Magus, Thatagus, Saka.

3. Says Darius the king there (was) one man Martiya by name, the son of Cicikhris—there (is) a town in Persia Kuganaka by name — here he halted; he rose up in Uvaja; thus he said to the state; I am Imanis king in Uvaja.

4. Says Darius the king then* I was near by Uvaja; afterwards from me . ... the people of Uvaja seized that Martiya who was chief of them and slew him.

---

*Old Persian ADa .IY For various theories respecting the meaning and derivation of ADaKaIY, cf F Muller (Wiener Zeitschrift fur d k. des Morgenlandes III), 150, Bartholomæ (Bezz Beiter X 272) The theory contained in a late number of the Zeitschr f vergl Sprchfg. is especially deserving of mention The first element of the compound is ADa (Cf Skt ADHa, Lat inde, Gr ἔνθα) and the second contains the stem of the interrogative pronoun, Ka, (Cf Skt ca, Lat que, Gr τε). Cf. Lat. TUN-C. „Den indefiniten und enclitischen gebrauch des fragestamms finden wir abgesehen von andern sprachen (z. b gr. ποί, πη) auch im apers ciy (*qid), welches einerseits den interrogativstamm selbst indefinit macht (kashsciy), andererseits adverb eine indefinite nebenbedeutung verleiht (paruvamciy „früher ') Genau wie das eben angeführte paruvamciy ist unser adakaiy gebildet. das dem -ciy entsprechende kaiy hat nur eine andere casusform. Deren locativische function ist bewahrt („in einem gewissen punkte"), hat aber in verbindung mit der zeitpartikel eine temporale bedeutungsmodification erhalten ada-kaiy bedeutet demnach „da zu einer gewissen zeit" „da einmal" d i , damals " Die deutsche partikel „'damals" und adakaiy stimmen also nicht nur in der bedeutung, sondern auch in der bildungsweise und bedeutungsentwicklung vollkommen überein."

5. Says Darius the king one man Fravartis by name, a Mede, he rose up in Media; thus he said to the state; I am Khshathrita of the family of Uvakhshatara; afterwards the Median state which was in clans became estranged from me (and) went over to that Fravartis; he became king in Media.

6. Says Darius the king the Persian and Median army, which was by him, it was faithful ? (lit. a faithful (?) thing); afterwards I sent forth an army; Vidarna* by name, a Persian, my subject him I made chief of them; thus I said to them; go smite that Median army which does not call itself mine; afterwards this Vidarna with the army went away; when he came to Media . . . . . . there (is) a town in Media . . . . . . by name — here he engaged in battle with the Medes; he who was chief among the Medes did not then hold (the army) faithful ?; Auramazda bore me aid; by the grace of Auramazda the army of Vidarna smote that rebellious army utterly; on the 6th day of the month Anamaka then it was the battle (was) thus fought by them; afterwards my army — there (is) a region Ka(m)pada by name — there awaited me until I went to Media.

7. Says Darius the king afterwards Dadarsis by name, an Armenian, my subject, him I sent forth to Armenia; thus I said to him; go, the rebellious army which does not call itself mine smite it; afterwards Dadarsis went away; when he came to Armenia, afterwards the rebellious ones having come together went against Dadarsis to engage in battle . . . . a village . . . . . . by name in Armenia; here they engaged in battle; Auramazda bore me aid; by the grace of Auramazda my army smote that rebellious army utterly; on the 6th day of the month Thuravahara then it was thus the battle (was) fought by them.

---

*Cf Grammar, 61, A, and note 1.

8. Says Darius the king a second time the rebellious ones having come together went against Dadarsis to engage in battle; there (is) a stronghold, Tigra by name, in Armenia — here they engaged in battle; Auramazda bore me aid; by the grace of Auramazda, my army smote that rebellious army utterly; on the 18th day of the month, Thuravahara then it was the battle (was) thus fought by them.

9. Says Darius the king a third time the rebellious ones having come together went against Dadarsis to engage in battle; there (is) a stronghold, U....ama by name, in Armenia — here they engaged in battle; Auramazda bore me aid; by the grace of Auramazda my army smote that rebellious army utterly; on the 9th day of the month, Thaigarcis then it was thus the battle (was) fought by them; afterwards Dadarsis awaited me until I came to Media.

10. Says Darius the king afterwards Vaumisa by name, a Persian, my subject, him I sent forth to Armenia; thus I said to him; go, the rebellious army which does not call itself mine, smite it; afterwards Vaumisa went away; when he came to Armenia afterwards, the rebellious ones having come together went against Vaumisa to engage in battle; there (is) a region, ... by name, in Assyria—here they engaged in battle; Auramazda bore me aid; by the aid of Auramazda my army smote that rebellious army utterly; on the 15th day of the month Anamaka, then it was thus the battle (was) fought by them.

11. Says Darius the king a second time the rebellious ones having come together went against Vaumisa to engage in battle; there (is) a region Autiyara by name in Armenia—here they engaged in battle; Auramazda bore me aid; by the grace of Auramazda my army smote that rebellious army utterly; .... of the month Thuravahara ...... thus the battle

(was) fought by them; afterwards Vaumisa awaited me in Armenia until I came to Media.

12. Says Darius the king afterwards I went from Babylon; I went away to Media; when I went to Media—there (is) a town Kudurus by name in Media —here this Fravartis (i. e., Phaortes) who called himself king in Media went with (his) army against me to engage in battle; afterwards we engaged in battle; Auramazda bore me aid; by the grace of Auramazda I smote the army of Fravartis utterly; on the 26th day of the month Adukanis then it was we engaged in battle.

13. Says Darius the king afterwards this Fravartis with faithful ? horsemen—in that place (was) a region Raga by name in Media—here went; afterwards I sent forth my army against them; Fravartis was seized (and) led to me; I cut off (his) nose and ears and tongue, and to him .... I led; he was held bound at my court; the whole state saw him; afterwards I put (him) on a cross at Ecbatana, and what men were his foremost allies, these I threw within a prison at Ecbatana.

14. Says Darius the king one man, Citra(n)takhma by name, a Sagartian, he became rebellious to me; thus he said to the state; I am king in Sagartia, of the family of Uvakhshatara; afterwards I sent forth the Persian and Median army; Takhmaspada by name, a Mede, my subject, him I made chief of them; thus I said to them; go, the rebellious army, which does not call itself mine, smite it; afterwards Takhmaspada went away with the army (and) engaged in battle with Citra(n)takhma; Auramazda bore me aid; by the grace of Auramazda my army smote that rebellious army utterly and seized Citra(n)takhma (and) brought (him) to me; afterwards I cut off his nose and ears, and to him ..... I led, he was held bound at my

court; the whole state saw him; afterwards I put him on a cross in Arabia.

15. Says Darius the king this (is) what (was) done by me in Media.

16. Says Darius the king Parthia and Hyrcania .... of Fravartis .... called himself; Hystaspes my father .... army .... afterwards Hystaspes . . . allies .... town . . . by name ...... they engaged in battle................thus the battle (was) fought by them.

III.

1. Says Darius the king afterwards I sent forth the Persian army to Hystaspes from Raga; when this army came to Hystaspes, afterwards Hystaspes with that army went away—there (is) a town Patigrabana by name in Parthia—here he engaged in battle with the rebellious ones; Auramazda bore me aid; by the grace of Auramazda Hystaspes smote that rebellious army utterly; on the first day of the month Garmapada then it was that thus the battle (was) fought by them.

2. Says Darius the king afterwards it became my province; this (is) what (was) done by me in Parthia.

3. Says Darius the king there (is) a region Margus by name; it became rebellious to me; one man Frada, a Margianian, him they made chief; afterwards I sent forth Dadarsis by name, a Persian, my subject, satrap in Bactria against him; thus I said to him: go, smite that army which does not call itself mine; afterwards Dadarsis with the army went away (and) engaged in battle with the Margianians; Auramazda bore me aid; by the grace of Auramazda my army smote that rebellious army utterly; on the 23rd day of the month Atriyadiya then it was thus the battle (was) fought by them.

4. Says Darius the king afterwards it became my province; this (is) what (was) done by me in Bactria.

5. Says Darius the king one man Vahyazdata by name—there (is) a town Tarava by name; there (is) a region Yutiya by name in Persia—here halted; he a second time (i. e., after Gaumata) rose up in Persia; thus he said to the state; I am Bardiya the son of Cyrus; afterwards the Persian army which (was) in clans departed from duty; it became estranged from me (and) went over to that Vahyazdata; he became king in Persia.

6. Says Darius the king afterwards I sent forth the

Persian and Median army which was by me; Artavardiya by name, a Persian, my subject, him I made chief of them; the other Persian army went with (lit. after) me to Media; afterwards Artavardiya with the army went to Persia; when he came to Persia—there (is) a town Rakha by name in Persia—here this Vahyazdata who called himself Bardiya went with (his) army against Artavardiya to engage in battle; afterwards they engaged in battle; Auramazda bore me aid; by the grace of Auramazda my army smote that army of Vahyazdata utterly; on the 12th day of the month Thuravahara then it was thus the battle (was) fought by them.

7. Says Darius the king afterwards this Vahyazdata with faithful? horsemen then went to Paishiyauvada; from thence he went with an army again against Artavardiya to engage in battle; there (is) a mountain Paraga by name—here they engaged in battle; Auramazda gave me aid; by the grace of Auramazda my army smote that army of Vahyazdata utterly; on the 6th day of the month Garmapada then it was thus the battle (was) fought by them and they seized that Vahyazdata and what men were his foremost allies, they seized.

8. Says Darius the king afterwards—there (is) a a town is Persia Uvadaidaya by name*—here, that Vahyazdata and what men were his foremost allies, them I put on a cross.

9. Says Darius the king this Vahyazdata who called himself Bardiya he sent forth an army to Harauvatis —there (was) Vivana by name, a Persian, my subject, satrap in Harauvatis—against him (he sent an army)

*The reader has noticed the constant use of paratax. Instead of bringing the words of the sentence into syntax independent constructions are employed. In no other language is this loose arrangement (which we must feel was original to speech) shown to better advantage than in the old Persian inscriptions. Cf Grammar, 59.

and one man he made chief of them; thus he said to them: go, smite that Vivana and that army which calls itself of Darius the king, afterwards this army, which Vahyazadata sent forth, went against Vivana, to engage in battle; there is a stronghold Kapishakanis by name—here they engaged in battle; Auramazda bore me aid; by the grace of Auramazda my army smote that rebellious army utterly; on the 13th day of the month Anamaka then it was thus the battle (was) fought by them.

10. Says Darius the king again the rebellious ones having come together went against Vivana to engage in battle; there (is) a region Ga(n)dutava by name—here they engaged in battle; Auramazda bore me aid; by the grace of Auramazda my army smote that rebellious army utterly; on the 8th day of the month Viyakhna then it was thus the battle (was) fought by them.

11. Says Darius the king afterwards this man, who was chief of that army which Vahyazdata sent against Vivana, this chief with faithful ? horseman went away —there (is) a stronghold Arshada by name in Harauvatis—he went beyond thence; afterwards Vivana, with an army on foot went (against) them; here he seized him and what men were his foremost allies he slew.

12. Says Darius the king afterwards the province became mine; this is what was done by me at Harauvatis.

13. Says Darius the king when I was in Persia and Media a second time the Babylonians became estranged from me; one man, Arakha by name, an Armenian son of Han(?)dita,* he rose up in Babylon;

*The N in Handita as well as the N in Dubana conjecture has supplied. The combination of wedges in the cuneiform text resembles no other characters on the stone and perhaps is the sign for L which otherwise would be wanting in the Old Persian alphabet. I, however, feel that it is simply a careless writing of the nasal.

there (is) a region, Duban(?)a by name—from there he rose up; thus he lied; I am Nabukudracara, the son of Nabunita; afterwards the Babylonian state became estranged from me (and) went over to that Arakha; he seized Babylon; he became king in Babylon.

14. Says Darius the king afterwards I sent forth my army to Babylon; Vi(n)dafra by name, a Mede, my subject, him I made chief; thus I said to them; go, smite that army in Babylon which does not call itself mine; afterwards Vi(n)dafra with an army went to Babylon; Auramazda bore me aid; by the grace of Auramazda, Vi(n)dafra seized Babylon........... on the 2d day of the month......then it was thus...
....
....
....

IV.

1. Says Darius the king this (is) what was done by me in Babylon.

2. Says Darius the king this (is) what I did; by the grace of Auramazda it was (done) wholly in (my) way;* after that the kings became rebellious I engaged in XIX battles; by the grace of Auramazda I smote them† and I seized IX kings; there was one, Gaumata by name, a Magian; he lied; thus he said; I am Bardiya the son of Cyrus; he made Persia rebellious; there (was) one, Atrina by name, in Uvaja; he lied; thus he said; I am king in Uvaja; he made Uvaja rebellious to me; there (was) one, Naditabira by name, a Babylonian; he lied; thus he said; I am Nabukudracara the son of Nabunita; he made Babylon rebellious; there (was) one, Martiya by name, a Persian; he lied; thus he said; I am Imanis king in Uvaja; he made Uvaja rebellious; there (was) one Fravartis by name, a Mede; he lied; thus he said; I am Khshathrita of the family of Uvakhshatara; he made Media rebellious; there (was) one, Citra(n)takhma by name, in Sagartia; he lied; thus he said; I am King in Sagartia, of the family of Uvakhshatara; he made Sagartia rebellious; there (was) one, Frada by name, a Margianian; he lied; thus he said; I am a king in Margus, he made Margus rebellious; there (was) one, Vahyazdata by name, a Persian; he lied; thus he said; I am Bardiya the son of Cyrus; he made Persia rebellious; there (was) one, Arakha by name, an Armenian; he lied; thus he said; I am Nabukudracara the son of Nabunita; he made Babylon rebellious.

---

*HAMAHYAYA THARDA is of doubtful interpetation. Rawl suggested "the performance of the whole", Oppert "dans toute ma vie; dans toute l'annie, toujours"; Spiegel "in aller Weiser." Many attempts have been made to connect THARDA with the Sanskrit ÇARAD, *autumn* used in the Veda metaphorically for *year*. Cf Grammar, 80, c.

† Or *smote theirs*, i. e., their forces Cf. Grammar, 83, B.

3. Says Darius the king these IX kings I seized within these battles.

4. Says Darius the king these (are) the provinces which became rebellious; a lie made them*....that these deceived the state; afterwards Auramazda made them in my hand; as desire (moved) me, thus.......

5. Says Darius the king O thou who wilt be king in the future, protect thyself strongly from deceit; whatever man will be a deceiver, him punish well (lit. him well punished punish. Cf., I. 8), if thus thou shalt think "may my country be firm."

6. Says Darius the king this (is) what I did; by the grace of Auramazda I did (it) wholly in (my) way;† O thou who shalt examine this inscription in the future, let it convince thee (as to) what (was) done by me; do not deceive thyself.

7. Says Darius the king Auramazda (is) a witness? that this (is) true (and) not false (which) I did wholly in my way.‡

8. Says Darius the king by the grace of Auramazda ....(what) else (was) done by me to a great extent, that (is) not inscribed on this inscription; for this reason it (is) not inscribed lest whoever will examine this inscription in the future.............. it may not convince him (as to) what (was) done by me (and) he may think (it) false.§

9. Says Darius the king who were the former kings, by these nothing (was) done to a great extent as (was)

---

*Perhaps we can supply with Spiegel HAMITRIYA *a lie made them rebellious*

†Cf. IV. 2.

‡Cf IV. 2.

§Although much has become obliterated yet we have enough to enable us to gain the sense of the passage. The idea is: should I write the memorial of all my achievements, they would be so many that men would lose faith in the testimony of this stone.

performed* wholly by me through the grace of Auramazda.

10. Says Darius the king..........let it convince thee (as to) what (was) done by me; thus.......... for this reason do not hide (this monument); if thou shalt not hide this monument (but) tell (it) to the state, may Auramazda be a friend to thee and may there be to thee a family abundantly and live thou long.

11. Says Darius the king if thou shalt hide this monument (and) not tell (it) to the state, may Auramazda be a smiter to thee and may there not be to thee a family.

12. Says Darius the king this (is) what I did wholly in (my) way;† by the grace of Auramazda I did (it); Auramazda bore me aid and the other gods which are.

13. Says Darius the king for this reason Auramazda bore me aid and the other gods which are, because I was not an enemy, I was not a deceiver, I was not a despot................family above law, above me ....I did......that whoever for me helped those belonging to my race, him well supported I supported; whenever..............him well punished I punished.

14. Says Darius the king O thou who art king in the future, whatever man shall be a deceiver........ shall be..........(be) not a friend to these; punish these with severe punishment.

15. Says Darius the king O thou who shalt see this inscription in the future which I inscribed or these pictures, thou shalt not destroy (them)‡ as long as thou shalt live; thus guard them.

---

*Cf. IV. 2, but here THARDA fails to appear.

†Cf. IV. 2.

‡Old Persian YAVA. „Für das auffällige —a scheinen mir und zwei möglichkeiten offen: es konnte yava nach abfall des t als flectierbarer a-stamm vom sprachgefühl aufgefasst an das femininum tauma sich formell anschliessen (mit einbusse der conjunctionalen bedeutung),

16. Says Darius the king if thou shalt see this inscription or these pictures (and) shalt not destroy them and shalt guard them for me as long as (thy) family shall be, may Auramazda be a friend to thee and may there be to thee a family abundantly and live thou long and whatever thou shalt do, this for thee (let) Auramazda......let him grant thy prayers.

19. Says Darius the king if thou shalt see this inscription or these pictures (and) shalt destroy them and shalt not guard them for me as long as (thy) family shall be, may Auramazda be a smiter to thee and may there not be to thee a family and whatever thou shalt do this let Auramazda destroy for thee.

18. Says Darius the king these (are) the men who were there then when I slew Gaumata the Magian who called himself Bardiya; then these men co-operated as my allies; Vi(n)dafrana by name, the son of Vayaspara, a Persian; Utana by name, the son of Thukhra, a Persian; Gaubaruva by name, the son of Marduniya, a Persian; Vidarna by name, the son of Magabigna, a Persian; Bagabukhsha by name, the son of Daduhya, a Persian; Ardumanis by name, the son of Vahauka, a Persian.

19. Says Darius the king O thou who art king in the future, what............what Darius.............
....
....
.......................I did.

---

oder es hat nach analogie von yatha, yata („bis, wärend") und andern auf -a ausleutenden conjunctionen selbst langen auslaut erhalten

Wenn allerdings Bh IV, 71 yava ji[vahy] zu lesen ist, so bleibt die zweite erklärung allein übrig Die gegenseitige beeinflussung von partikeln bietet nichts auffallendes; es kann ἄνευς (Brugmann Griech. Gramm §200) neben ἄνευ, ngr ἀντίς neben ἀντί, τότες neben τότε u ä nach analogie von μέχρι-ς etc., sowie überhaupt das umsichgreifen des auslautenden -s in griech. partikeln (οὕτω-ς, ὥς, etc.) verglichen werden." (A. T.)

J Schmidt explains YAVA as neuter plural (172).

V.

1. Says Darius the king this (is) what I did...... .... way............. ....king.............province; this became estranged from me; one man ..imina by name; the (people) of Uvaja made him chief; afterwards I seut forth (my) army to Uvaja; one man Gaubaruva by name, a Persian, my subject, him I made chief of them; afterwards this Gaubaruva with an army went to Uvaja; he engaged in battle with the rebellious ones; afterwards .... and to him .... he seized and led to me.....................province............. .... thus it ....

2. Says Darius the king .... Auramazda .... by the grace of Auramazda................ I did.

3. Says Darius the king whoever in the future ....

4. Says Darius the King .... I went against Saka.......................... ....Tigris..............to the sea .... I seized the enemy .... to...... .... Saku(n)ka by name, him I seized .... there another as chief .... afterwards ....

5. Says Darius the king .... not Auramazda .... if by the grace of Auramazda .... I did.

6. Says Darius the king ...... worship? Auramazda ....

Kossowicz remarks: "Notatu dignum, omnium, quantum scio, imperatorum, qui armorum vi atque gloria celebres extiterant, nisi duo, Darium Hystaspi nempe et Napoleonem I — mum, commilitonum nomina; victorias suas recensendo, in publicis monumentis memoriae tradidisse."

The Smaller Inscriptions of Behistan.

a.

OVER THE PICTURE OF DARIUS.*

I (am) Darius, the great king, king of kings, king of Persia, king of the countries, the son of Hystaspes, the grandson of Arshama, the Achaemenide. Says Darius the king my father (is) Hystaspes, the father of Hystaspes (is) Arshama, the father of Arshama (is) Ariyaramna, the father of Ariyaramna (is) Caispis, the father of Caispis (is) Achaemenes. Says Darius the king therefore we are called Achaemenides; from long ago we have extended; from long ago our family have been kings. Says Darius the king VIII of my family (there were) who were formerly kings; I am the ninth IX; individually we are kings.

b.

UNDER THE PROSTRATE FORM.

This Gaumata the Median lied; thus he said; I am Bardiya, the son of Cyrus; I am king.

c.

OVER THE FIRST STANDING FIGURE.

This Atrina lied; thus he said; I am king in Uvaja.

d.

OVER THE SECOND STANDING FIGURE.

This Naditabira lied; thus he said; I am Nabuk(u)dracara, the son of Nabunita; I am king in Babylon.

e.

UPON THE GARMENT OF THE THIRD STANDING FIGURE.

This Fravartis lied; thus he said; I am Khshathrita of the family of Uvakhshatara; I am king in Media.

---

*Cf. I, 1-4.

f.

OVER THE FOURTH STANDING FIGURE.

This Martiya lied; thus he said; I am Imanis, king in Uvaja.

g.

OVER THE FIFTH STANDING FIGURE.

This Citra(n)takhma lied; thus he said; I am king in Sagartia, of the family of Uvakhshatara.

h.

OVER THE SIXTH STANDING FIGURE.

This Vahyazdata lied; thus he said; I am Bardiya, the son of Cyrus; I am king.

i.

OVER THE SEVENTH STANDING FIGURE.

This Arakha lied; thus he said; I am Nabuk(u)dracara, the son of Nabunita; I am king in Babylon.

j.

OVER THE EIGHTH STANDING FIGURE.

This Frada lied; thus he said; I am king in Margus.

k.

OVER THE NINTH STANDING FIGURE.*

This (is) Saku(n)ka, the Sakian.

---

*Herodotus mentions the high cap which was peculiar to the garb of the Sakians It is interesting to note that the figure is represented on the stone wearing this national head-dress.

The Inscription of Alvend. (O.)

(PERSIAN)

This inscription is engraven upon two niches on a large block of stone near the base of Mt. Alvend. Not only is the monumental fame of Darius perpetuated by the Behistan mountain, but in different parts of the Persian empire this monarch caused to be inscribed historic records of his reign. At Persepolis the palaces declare the name of their founder and his prayers for the protection of heaven. To Darius beyond all others we are indebted for what we have of the Paleography of Persia.

I TRANSLATION.

A great God (is) Auramazda who created this earth, who created yonder heaven,* who created man, who created the† spirit? of man, who made Darius king, one king of many, one lord of many. I (am) Darius the great king, king of kings, king of the countries possessing many kinds of people, king of this great earth far and wide, the son of Hystaspes, the Achæmenide.

---

*ASMAN (*heaven*) is literally *a stone* as we know from its cognate in Sanskrit. Probably the Persians regarded the sky as a solid dome; cf. the Hebrew word RAQI(A) (Gen. I. 8) and our *firmament* (firmamentum).

†The old Persian SHIYATIS is the Avest. SHAITI The Assyrian translates the word by DUMQU "blessing." But cf. Fick, idg. Wb. I[8] 233. and J. Schmidt Plur. d. idg. Ntr. 418.

The Inscriptions of Suez. (SZ.)

(PERSIAN, MEDIAN, ASSYRIAN, EGYPTIAN)

A crowned head is carved upon the stone together with the following legend:

TRANSLATION.

A.

Darius the great king; king of kings, king of the countries, the son of Hystaspes, the Achaemenide.

Above are a dozen lines of Persian cuneiform text the translation of which follows:

TRANSLATION.

B.

A great god (is) Auramazda, who created yonder heaven, who created this earth, who created man, who created the spirit*? of man, who made Darius king, who gave the kingdom to Darius; what great

. . . .

I (am) Darius the great king, king of kings, king of the countries possessing many people, king of this great earth far and wide, son of Hystaspes, the Achaemenide. Says Darius the king I am a Persian; with (the help of) Persia I seized Egypt; I commanded to dig this canal,† from the Nile by name a river which flows in Egypt, to the sea which goes from Persia; afterwards this canal was dug there as I commanded....

. . . .

. . . .

. . . .

---

*Cf note under (O)

†Cf. Herodotus, IV 39.

The Inscription of London.

(PERSIAN, MEDIAN, ASSYRIAN.)

The following short inscription can be seen in the British Museum on a cylinder which furnishes a fine specimen of gem engraving. A warrior in his chariot is represented as attacking at full speed a lion,* the symbol of power. This warrior from his crown we can interpret as King Darius. He holds his bow ready for action, while the charioteer urges on the steeds. This cylinder was carried to England from Egypt.

TRANSLATION.

I (am) Darius the king.

---

*On the Persian sculptures, the lion and bull occur often, as emblems of strength. Metaphors of this kind are frequent in all oriental literature. In making a list of the epithets of the god Indra in the Veda, one is struck with the repeated comparisons of this sort However, the Vedic poets drew from the stall as the most fertile source of metaphors, and it was the later Sanskrit which used the beasts of the forest more extensively for that purpose. (e. g., the tiger of men, etc) In Biblical literature the reader is referred to Ezekiel i 10. "As for the likeness of their faces, they four had the faces of man, and the face of a lion on the right side." Daniel vii. 4. "The first was like a lion and had eagles' wings" The familiar national emblems of later date, the Roman eagle, the British lion, etc., all had their origin in this early conception.

The Inscriptions of Darius at Persepolis.

(PERSIAN, [MEDIAN, ASSYRIAN.])

The inscriptions of Persepolis show that same spirit of patriotism which characterizes the record on Mt. Behistan. The superiority of Persia over the provinces of the empire is set forth by the monarch with the purpose of elevating the feelings of his countrymen and of keeping alive ever in their hearts the love of country. The palace of Darius shows the ruins of several departments with external chambers which were evidently guard-rooms. The roof of a large room, fifty feet square, was supported by pillars, the bases of which remain to-day. This edifice is one of those ruins which represent the combined work of several successive Achaemenian kings. All the structures stand upon the same platform around which are great walls of hewn stone. Two inscriptions are found above the wall and one on two pillars, which read as follows:

TRANSLATION.

H.

ABOVE THE WALL SURROUNDING THE PALACE.

The great Auramazda, who (is) the greatest of the gods, he made Darius king; he gave to him the kingdom; by the grace of Auramazda Darius (is) king. Says Darius the king this (is) the country Persia which Auramazda gave me, which, beautiful, possessing good horses, possessing good men, by the grace of Auramazda and (by the achievements) of me Darius the king, does not fear an* enemy. (?) Says Darius the king let Auramazda bear me aid with (his) fellow gods and let Auramazda protect this country from an army, from misfortune, from deceit; may not an enemy .... come unto this country, nor an army,

---

*Or, THE OTHER (i e., AHRIMAN) Cf. note to (I)

nor misfortune nor deceit; this I pray of Auramazda .... with (his) fellow gods; this let Auramazda give me with (his) fellow gods.

I.

ANOTHER INSCRIPTION ABOVE THE WALL.

I (am) Darius the great king, king of kings, king of many countries, the son of Hystaspes, the Achaemenide. Says Darius the king by the grace of Auramazda these (are) the provinces which I subdued with (the help of) that Persian army, (and) which feared me (and) brought to me tribute; Uvaja, Media, Babylon, Arabia, Assyria, Egypt, Armenia, Cappadocia, Sparda, Ionia, which (are) of the dry (land) (and) which (are) of the sea, and the provinces which (are) in the east, Sagartia, Parthia, Zara(n)ka, Haraiva, Bactria, Sugda, Uvarazamiya, Thatagus, Harauvatis, India, Ga(n)dara, Saka, Maka. Says Darius the king if thus thou shalt think "may I not fear an enemy,"* protect this Persian state; if the Persian state shall be protected, may this goddess (namely) this spirit (of patriotism) for a long time unharmed, descend upon this race.

B.

OVER THE PILLARS IN THE PALACE.

Darius the great king, king of kings, king of the countries, the son of Hystapes, the Achaemenide, who built this palace.

---

* Dr Julius Oppert understood the Old Persian word ANIYA (other) to be the only notion of AHRIMAN found in the inscriptions. He argued that the word ANIYA never means "enemy:" The prayer he translated "The good Principle, which has always destroyed the Hater (DUVAISATAM) will descend on this house."

The Inscription on the Tomb of Darius. (NR.)

(PERSIAN, MEDIAN, ASSYRIAN.)

Naqshi—Rustam is the burial place of Darius.

On the face of a mountain which rises to the perpendicular height of 900 feet are cut the excavations which are doubtless tombs. These relics have a common external appearance. They are carved into the rock fourteen feet deep in the form of a cross, the upright section of which is about ninety feet, the transverse division about fifty feet. Four pilasters about seven feet apart ornament the transverse section, in the midst of which is the door of the tomb. On the division above the façade of this sepulchre are the sculptures. A double row of fourteen figures supports two cornices. Two bulls form the pillars at each end of the upper cornice. On an elevated pedestal of three steps stands a figure dressed in a flowing robe, holding his bow in his left hand. Without doubt this is the effigy of him who lies buried beneath. Opposite the standing form, on a pedestal of three steps, is an altar, upon which the sacred fire is burning, while above is a disk, probably representing the sun, of which the fire blazing at the shrine is the symbol. Above is the image of Auramażda. One of these structures Ker-Porter visited, and with great difficulty explored its interior. Although he was not able to read the inscription, yet he conjectured that this was the tomb of Darius. I quote him at this point. "The second tomb is the only one whereon the marks of an inscription can be traced; but over the whole tablet of the upper compartment letters are visible wherever they could be introduced; above the figures, between them and the altar, along the side, from top to bottom; in short, everywhere we see it covered with the arrow-headed characters and in good preservation. What a treasure of information doubtless is there to the happy man who can decipher it. It was tantalizing to a painful degree to look at such a sealed book in the very spot of mystery, where probably its contents would explain all. But it certainly is a very distinguishing peculiarity of this tomb that it alone should contain any inscription, and that the writing on it is so abundant; a circumstance that might warrant the supposition of this being the tomb that was cut by the express orders of Darius Hystaspes to receive his remains." (Travels in Georgia, Persia, Armenia, ancient Babylonia, etc., etc., by Sir Robert Ker-Porter, vol. I, p. 523.)

Before translating the inscription I wish to call the attention of the reader to Herod. III, 88.

TRANSLATION.

A.

A great god is Auramazda, who created this earth, who created yonder heaven, who created man, who created the spirit* of man, who made Darius king, one king of many, one lord of many. I (am) Darius the great king, king of kings, king of the countries possessing many kinds of people, king of this great earth far and wide, son of Hystaspes the Achaemenide, a Persian, the son of a Persian: an Aryan, an Aryan offspring. Says Darius the king by the grace of Auramazda these (are) the provinces which I seized afar† from Persia; I ruled them; they brought tribute to me .... what was commanded to them by me, this they did; the law which (is) mine that was established; Media, Uvaja, Parthia, Haraiva, Bactria, Suguda, Uvarazamis, Zara(n)ka Harauvatis, Thatagus, Ga(n)dara, India, Sakae, Humavarkae, Sakae Tigrakhaudae, Babylon, Assyria, Arabia, Egypt, Armenia,

*Cf. note to (O).

†Or, EXCEPT PERSIA.

SUPPLEMENTARY NOTE TO NRa.

As this volume goes to press an article (published in 1893) comes from the pen of the distinguished scholar Hübschmann. He insists on "übel" as the signification of GaSTa (NRa) against Thumb's argument (published in 1891) which I have quoted at some length on p. 147. I add a few extracts.

"Auf diese erklärung Kern's greift nun A. Thumb zurück, ohne die gründe, die für Spiegel's deutung sprechen, zu erwägen. Diese gründe aber sind durchaus stichhaltig und werfen Thumb's erklärung um. GaSTa ist in der keilschrift 2. gattung durch ein wort übersetzt, das früher *siyunika*, von Oppert...... *visnika*, von Weisbach...... *mushnika* gelesen wird, dessen bedeutung aber nicht zweifelhaft ist......... und sein aequivalent im Babylonischen text ist *bi-i-shi*, das ,,böse'' bedeutet.*

Wie mit GaSTa, steht es auch mit THaDaYa; die alte erklärung† ist die richtige........Meine übersetzung lautete: O mensch, der befehl des Ahuramazda, er soll dir nicht übel erscheinen."‡

---

*BISHU seems to render into Assyrian the Persian ARIKa (ARaIKa) "enemy."

†i. e., As an augmentless imperfect third singular (Cf. Grammar 95B.) and connected with Avestan SaD "seem".

‡Cf. Oppert's translation of the Median "homo quae est Oromazis doctrina, illa tibi mala ne videatur". Also cf. translation of the Median given in foot note on p. 149.

Cappadocia, Sparda, Ionia, Sakae beyond the sea, the Ionians wearing long hair* Patians Kusians, Macians, Karkians. Says Darius the king Auramazda when he saw this earth .... afterwards gave it to me; he made me king; I am king; by the grace of Auramazda I established it on (its) foundation; what I commanded to them, this they did as desire came to (lit. was) me. If perchance thou shalt think that manifold (lit. a manifold thing) are these provinces which Darius the king held, look at the picture (of those) who are bearing my throne,† in order that thou mayest know them; then to thee will be the knowledge (that) the spear of a Persian man hath gone forth afar; then to thee will be the knowledge (that) a Persian man waged battle far from Persia. Says Darius the king this (is) what (was) done; all this by the grace of Auramazda I did; Auramazda bore me aid until this was done, let Auramazda protect me from .... and my race and this country; this I pray of Auramazda; this let Auramazda give me. O man, what (are) the commands of Auramazda, may he (make them) revealed to thee; do not err; do not leave the right path, do not sin.‡

---

*Cf. the Homeric καρηκομόωντες.

†The northern throne of the great palace contains five tiers of ten warriors supporting the platform on which the king is represented sitting, surrounded by his attendants.

‡Cf. Bartholomae Bezz. Beitr. X, 269, and Kern (ZDMG. XXIII, 222). For meaning of. MA STaRaVa, cf. Mélanges, Asiat III, 344. Thumb (Zeitschrift für vgl. Sprachforsch, 1891) translates „O mensch! lass dir die lehre des Auramazda gesagt sein. Verabscheue sie nicht den richtigen weg (d. h. die lehre des A.), beflecke ihn nicht " I quote an extract,

"Zunächst halte ich die erklärung von *gasta* als „stinkend — widerwärtig" wegen der merkwürdigen bedeutungsübertragung ins ethische für unwahrscheinlich und ziehe die von selbst sich aufdrängende zugehörigkeit zu ai. *gad* „sagen, sprechen" vor. Kern hat dies schon längst gesehen und in dem worte das part. auf *-ta* erkannt; aber bei einem transitiven verbum durch die annahme medialer bedeutung

B.

A great god (is) Auramazda who ....
......made spirit ? of man ....
above Darius the king ....
.... Says Darius the king
by the grace of Auramazda ....
....
....
..........is violence.......................
....
......violence.....................

---

jenes verbaladjectivs den activen sinn ,,(er) hat gesagt'' herauszubringen, ist nicht weniger gezwungen gasta ist regelmässiges passives particip und muss mit hya zusammenconstruiert werden, welches ich als optativ der copula (*siet) fasse Es ist daher zu übersetzen ,,möge dir gesagt sein die lehre des Auramazda,'' ,,lass dir gasagt sein,'' d h ,,halte fest an . . . ''. Einen optativ hat in hya schon Bopp (Lautsystem d apers p. 149) vermutet, wenn auch seine weitere erklärung eine ganz andere, verfehlte ist. Wir gewinnen durch die von uns vorgeschlagene constructionsweise eine genaue parallele zu J. 22 f hya duvaistam shiyatis akhsata· in beiden fällen ist hya von dem nachfolgenden passiven particip getrennt und das subject in die mitte genommen; nur der gebrauch des optativs ist verschieden An unserer stelle bezeichnet er den einer aufforderung fast gleichkommenden wunsch.

Eine gewisse wahrscheinlichkeit, dass hya das pronomen hya nicht sein kann, sehe ich in dem umstand, dass mit ausnahme des einen hya amakham tauma (in gleicher wiederholung Bh I 8 und A 12) die verbindung hya + genetiv + substantiv durchaus ungewönlich ist (Ein solches hya (oder tya) is dagagen beliebt zwischen subst. und nachfolgenden gen Bh. I, 85 89 95 II, 69. III, 38 Bh I, 69 71. II, 27. 35 40 46. 55)

Die positiv ausgedrückte aufforderung wird mit den folgenden injunctiven nochmals in negativer form wiederholt. Die alte erklärung von ma thadaya ist nun natürlich unmöglich geworden; es ist die 2. pers sing des injunctivs wie die folgenden formen auch. Ich ziehe thad zur ai. wurzel çad ,,abfallen'' und sehe dieselbe wurzel im german, hatjan ,,hassen'', für das man meines wissens noch keine anknüpfung in den verwandten sprachen gefunden hat (s. Kluge, Etym. Wb s v). Die bedeutungsentwicklung ist,,abfallen, verwerfen, verabscheuen, hassen'' An unserer stelle haben wir die wahl zu übersetzen ,,falle nicht ab'' oder ,,verabscheue nicht''. Im letzern falle bildet ap thad den übergang in der bedeutungsentwicklung von ai. çad zu german. hassen Die zweite bedeutung ,,verabscheuen'' darf auf grund des durch die medische übersetzung festgestellten sinns

C.

Gaubaruva, a Patisuvarian, spear-bearer of Darius the king.

D.

Aspacana, quiver-bearer?, a server of the arrows of Darius the king.

E.

This (is) a Macian.

---

vorgezogen werden, wärend ich andererseits die richtigheit meiner erklärung der ganzen stelle mit der med. und assyr. übersetzung mehr in übereinstimmung finde als die frühere interpretation: Med. quae Oromazdis doctrina eam ne malam putes. Assyr. ,,was Ormuzd befiehlt, lehne dich nicht dagogen auf" (Bezold).

Für ma st*a*r*a*v*a* scheint mir weder Bollensens übersetzung ,,falle nicht ab" noch Bartholomae's ähnliche ,,verliere, verlasse nicht den pfad" genügend von den vorhergehended aufforderungen sich abzuheben, und ich halte daher Bartholomae's zweiten vorschlag ,,beflecke ihn (den pfad) nicht" (zu avest. a-star*a*ieti) für richtiger." For Thumbs' connection between O. P. th*a*d and Skt. çad, cf. Brugmann, Grunde. I, 397.

THE INSCRIPTIONS OF XERXES AT PERSEPOLIS.

(PERSIAN, MEDIAN, ASSYRIAN.)

TRANSLATION.

D.

UPON EACH ONE OF THE FOUR PILLARS OF THE ENTRANCES TO THE PALACE OF XERXES.

A great god (is) Auramazda who created this earth, who created yonder heaven, who created man, who created the spirit? of man, who created Xerxes king, one king of many, one lord of many. I (am) Xerxes the great king, king of kings, king of the countries, possessing many kinds of people, king of this great earth far and wide, the son of Darius the king, the Achaemenide. Says Xerxes the great king by the grace of Auramazda, this entrance possessing all countries I made; much else (that is) beautiful (was) done by* this Persian (people) which I did and which my father did; whatever (that has been) done seems beautiful, all that we did by the grace of Auramazda. Says Xerxes the king let Auramazda protect me and my kingdom and what (was) done by me and what (was) done by my father, (all) this let Auramazda protect.

G.

UPON THE PILLARS ON THE WESTERN SIDE OF THE PALACE, WHERE XERXES IS REPRESENTED STANDING WITH TWO ATTENDANTS.

Xerxes the great king, king of kings, the son of Darius the king, the Achaemenide.

*I have followed the old interpretation, (Cf. Oppert, Journal Asiat. XIX, 177 "avec cette Perse, aidé par ce peuple Perse"). If we can regard ana as the equivalent of the Avest. prep. *ana* (cf. Gr. ἀνα) we can translate "through Persia" (Parsa being the instr. sing. or better acc. plr.; Cf. Grammar, 86, B Note 1.) Cf. Zeitschrift für vergleichende Sprachforschung. p. 127 [1891]).

Ea.

UPON THE WALL BY THE STAIRS OF THE PALACE.

A great god (is) Auramazda who created this earth, who created yonder heaven, who created man, who created the spirit? of man, who made Xerxes king, one king of many, one lord of many. I (am) Xerxes the great king, king of kings, king of the provinces possessing many kinds of people, king of this great earth far and wide, son of Darius the king, the Achaemenide. Says Xerxes the great king by the grace of Auramazda this palace (lit. seat) I made; let Auramazda protect me with the gods and my kingdom and what (was) done by me.

Eb.

The above inscription is repeated on the western stairs of the palace.

Ca.

UPON THE HIGHEST PILLAR NEAR THE SOUTHERN STAIRS.

A great god (is) Auramazda who created this earth, who created yonder heaven, who created man, who created the spirit? of man, who made Xerxes king, one king of many, one lord of many. I (am) Xerxes the great king, king of kings, king of the provinces possessing many kinds of people, king of this great earth far and wide, son of Darius the king, the Achaemenide. Says Xerxes the great king by the grace of Aura* Mazda this palace (lit. seat) Darius the king made who (was) my father; let Auramazda protect me with the gods and what (was) done by my father Darius the king, (all) this let Auramazda protect with the gods.

---

*Notice that the two members of the compound are separated. Cf. Original Text of the Inscriptions.

Cb.

The above inscription is repeated upon the walls of the southern stairs.

A.

UPON THE STAIRS OF THE PALACE.

A great god (is) Auramazda who created this earth, who created yonder heaven, who created man, who created the spirit ? of man, who made Xerxes king, one king of many, one lord of many. I (am) Xerxes the great king, king of kings, king of the provinces possessing many kinds of people, king of this great earth far and wide, the son of Darius the king, the Achaemenide. Says Xerxes the great king what (was) done by me here and what (was) done by me afar, all this I did by the grace of Auramazda; let Auramazda protect me with the gods and my kingdom and what (was) done by me.

The Inscription of Xerxes at Alvend.

(PERSIAN, MEDIAN, ASSYRIAN.)

F.

The following inscription is engraven upon two niches cut into a small rock:

TRANSLATION.

A great god (is) Auramazda, who (is) greatest of the gods, who created this earth, who created yonder heaven, who created man, who created the spirit? of man, who made Xerxes king, one king of many, one lord of many. I (am) Xerxes the great king, king of kings, king of the provinces possessing many kinds of people, king of this great earth far and wide, the son of Darius the king, the Achaemenide.

The Inscription upon the Vase of Count Caylus.

(PERSIAN, MEDIAN, ASSYRIAN, EGYPTIAN.)

Qa.

This vase contains the three customary forms of cuneiform writing and a line of Egyptian hieroglyphics. The relic is preserved in Paris. Four fragments of similar alabaster vases containing the same quadrilingual inscription have been found by W. K. Loftus in Susa, and are to be seen to-day in the British Museum.

TRANSLATION.

I (am) Xerxes, the great king.

The Inscription at Van.

K.

(PERSIAN, MEDIAN, ASSYRIAN.)

This inscription is about sixty feet from the plain below, engraven upon a niche in an enormous rock which rises to the perpendicular height of one hundred feet.

TRANSLATION.

A great god (is) Auramazda who (is) the greatest of [the gods, who created this earth, who created yonder heaven, who created man, who created the spirit? of man, who made Xerxes king, one king of many, one lord of many. I (am) Xerxes the great king, king of kings, king of the provinces possessing many kinds of people, king of this great earth far and wide, the son of Darius the king, the Achaemenide. Says Xerxes the king, Darius, the king who (was) my father, he by the grace of Auramazda did what (was) beautiful to a great extent, and he commanded to carve this place ——? he did not make the inscriptions inscribed; afterwards I commanded to inscribe this inscription; (let Auramazda protect me with the gods and my kingdom and what (has been) done by me.*)

---

*Supplied from the Assyrian version.

THE INSCRIPTION OF ARTAXERXES I. (Qb)

(PERSIAN. MEDIAN, ASSYRIAN, EGYPTIAN.)

This inscription, which is quadrilingual is engraven upon a vase which is preserved in the treasury of St. Mark's at Venice.

TRANSLATION.

Artaxerxes,* the great king.

*The cuneiform text spells the name of the monarch on the vase ARDAKHCASHCA This spelling must be due either to foreign pronunciation or to the ignorance of the workman. Elsewhere the cuneiform characters given the regular ARTAKHSHATRA. Cf. Original Text of the Inscriptions.

THE INSCRIPTION OF DARIUS II. (L.)

(PERSIAN, MEDIAN, ASSYRIAN.)

TRANSLATION.

ABOVE THE POSTS OF THE WINDOWS IN THE PALACE AT PERSEPOLIS.

(This) lofty stone structure (has been) made by (one belonging to) the race of Darius the king.*

---

*The Median and Assyrian translate the last of this legend "in the house of Darius the king."

THE INSCRIPTION OF ARTAXERXES MNEMON AT SUSA.

(PERSIAN, MEDIAN, ASSYRIAN.)

This inscription is upon the base of one of the columns in the ruins of what once must have been a great palace. Much of this building was used for the pavement of other edifices by the races which in after time possessed this spot.

TRANSLATION.

a.

I (am) Artaxerxes, the great king, king of kings, the son of Darius* the king.

b.

UPON THE BASE OF THE PILLARS IN THE LARGE ROW OF COLUMNS.

This palace seems to have been fashioned after the model of that of Darius at Persepolis. In connection with this edifice it is interesting to refer to Dan. viii. 2. "And it came to pass when I saw, that I was in Susa (or Shushan) in the palace," etc.

TRANSLATION.

Says Artaxerxes the great king, king of kings, king of the countries, king of the earth, the son of Darius the king; Darius (was) the son of Artaxerxes the king; Artaxerxes (was) the son of Xerxes the king: Xerxes (was) the son of Darius the king; Darius (was) the son of Hystaspes, the Achaemenide; this building Darius, my ancestor made................ ......Artaxerxes (my) grandfather......Anakata and Mithra........by the grace of Auramazda the building I made; let Auramazda, Anahata and Mithra protect me........

*Cf. Grammar, 24. DARAYAVA(H)USH (Darius) although having a stem in U is treated like nouns whose stems end in *a*. So in Prakrit there is a strong tendency for the so-called first declension to trespass upon the others, thus breaking down the barriers which were observed by the Sanskrit.

THE INSCRIPTION OF ARTAXERXES OCHUS AT PERSEPOLIS. (P.)

(PERSIAN.)

TRANSLATION.

UPON THE STEPS OF THE PALACE.

A great god (is) Auramazda who created this earth, who created yonder heaven, who created man, who created the spirit? of man, who made me, Artaxerxes, king, one king of many, one lord of many. Says Artaxerxes the great king, king of kings, king of countries, king of the earth. I (am) the son of Artaxerxes, the king; Artaxerxes (was) the son of Darius the king; Darius (was) the son of Artaxerxes the king; Artaxerxes (was) the son of Xerxes the king; Xerxes (was) the son of Darius the king; Darius was the son of Hystaspes by name; Hystaspes was the son of Arshama by name, the Achaemenide. Says Artaxerxes the king this lofty stone structure (was) made by me during my reign (lit. under me). Says Artaxerxes the king let Auramazda and the god Mithra protect me and this country and what (was) done by me.

THE INSCRIPTION OF ARSACES.

(PERSIAN.)

TRANSLATION.

UPON THE SEAL OF GROTEFEND.

R.

Arsaces by name, son of Athiyabaushana.

PERSIAN-ENGLISH

VOCABULARY.

VOCABULARY.

For the sake of convenience in comparison, the same method of transliteration is adopted for Sanskrit and Avestan words as for Old Persian.

A.

A,—prefix, *to.* Skt., a; Avest., a; Lat. a(?) 'from'. (For postpositive a, cf. Bezz. Beitr. XIII.)

Ai,—pron. root in ait*a*, aiv*a*.

Ait*a*,—n. pr., *this*, *that.* Skt. et*a*t; Avest., aet*a*d; Lat., iste; Goth., thata; Eng., that.

Ain*a*,—name of the father of Naditabira.

Aiv*a*,—*one.* Skt., ek*a*; Avest., aev*a*.

Autiyar*a*,—name of a country in Armenia.

Aur*a* or A(h)ur*a*,—1) m., *master, ruler*; 2) f., *goddess.* Skt., asur*a*; Avest., ahur*a*.

Aur*a*m*a*zda or A(h)ur*a*m*a*zda,— the name of the greatest deity. Aur*a*, see above; m*a*zda, compound of m*az*, great: Skt., m*a*h*a*t; Lat., magnus; Goth., mag; AS., magan; Eng., might; and da, give: Skt., da; Avest., da; Lat., do: or da, know.

Akhsh,—*to see.* Skt., akshi; Lat., oc-ulus. (Cf. Paul Kretschmer in Zitsch. für vergl. Sprachforsch, p. 432 [1891]).

— with p*a*ti, *to oversee, rule.*

Akhsh*a*ta,—*whole, entire, perfect.* Fem. of an adjective, akhsh*ata*. Skt., aksh*ata*.

Ag*a*ta,— nomen agentis; *comer, friend*(?). Cf. g*a*m.

Aj(?),— *drive, do.* Skt., aj; Lat., ago. (It is possible to refer aj*a*t*a* to j*a*n, smite.)

Atiy,— verbal prefix, *beyond, across.* Skt.. ati; Lat., et; Old German, anti(?); Germ., und(?); Eng., and(?).

Ath*a*(n)gain*a*,— *stony, built of stone.*

Athura,— *Assyria.*

Atrin*a*,— proper name.

Atriyadiy*a*,— name of a month.

Ad*a*,— *then, thereupon.*

Ad*a*k*a*iy,— *then.*

Ad*a*m,— *I.* Skt., ah*a*m; Avest., azem; Lat., ego; Goth., ik; AS., ik or I; Eng., I. (For kh in amakham, cf. idg. Forschungen, p. 186 [1892]; for position of m*a*iy and mam, cf. Wackernagel, über ein Gesetz der idg. Wortstell, ibid.).

Aduk*a*nish.— name of a month.

An*a*h*a*t*a*,— Genius of the waters.

Anam*a*k*a*.— name of a month.

Aniy*a*,— 1) indef. pron., *another*; 2) *enemy?* Skt., any*a*; Avest., any*a*.

Anuv,— prep. with loc., *along, by.* Skt., anu.

Anushiy*a*,— *follower.* See anuv and shiyu; cf. Lat., comes (con-eo).

A(n)t*a*r,— prep. with acc., *within, in.* Skt., ant*a*r; Avest., ant*a*re; Lat., inter; Goth., undar.

Ap*a*,— verbal prefix, *from.* Skt., ap*a*; Avest., ap*a*; Lat., ab; Goth., af; Eng., of.

Ap*a*t*a*r*a*,— *remote, another.* Comparative of ap*a*.

Apadana,—*work, temple, building.*

Apanyaka,—*ancestor.*

Aparam,—adv., *afterward.*

Apariy,—*near by.*

Api,—*water.* Skt., ap; Avest., ap.

Apiy,—*to, also.* Skt., api; Avest., api.

Abacarish,—*commerce.*

Abashta,—*law.*

Abiy,—prep. with acc., *to, against.* Skt., abhi; Avest., aibiy; Lat., ob(?), ambi.

Abish,—prep. with loc., *by, at.*

Amutha,—*there, then.* Skt., amutra.

Ayadana,—acc. pl., ayadana, *sanctuaries, homes.*

Ayasta,—adv. or prep. with acc., *according to, with, unto* (?).

Arakadrish,—name of a Persian mountain.

Arakha,—name of an Armenian.

Arabaya,—1) *Arabian*; 2) *Arab, Arabia.*

Arika,—*enemy.* Skt., ari.

Ariya,—1) *Aryan*; 2) *noble.* Skt., arya; Avest., airya; New Persian, Iran; Keltic, erin; Eng., Ir-ish.

Ariyaramna or Ariyaramna,—name of the great-grandfather of Darius. Ariya and ram, to rejoice. (For change of stem, cf. Bartholomae, idg. Forsch., p. 180 [1892]).

Aruvastam (?)

Artakhshatra,—*Artaxerxes.* Arta (Avest., areta), lifted up; and khshatra, kingdom.

Art*a*v*a*rdiy*a*,— name of one of the commanders of Darius Hystaspes.

Ard*a*khc*a*shch*a*,— name of Artaxerxes as pronounced by the Egyptians.

Ard*a*stan*a*,— *high structure.*

Ardum*a*nish,— name of one of the Persians who swore with Darius against Smerdis.

Arbira,— *Arbela*; a city upon the confines of Media.

Arm*a*niy*a*,— 1) *Armenian*; 2) *Armenia.*

Armin*a*,— name of Armenia.

Arminiy*a*,— *Armenian.*

Arsh*a*k*a*,— *Arsaces.*

Arshada,— name of a fortress in Arachasia.

Arsham*a*,— name of the grandfather of Darius Hystaspes.

Arshtish,— *spear.* Skt., ṛshti; Avest., arsti.

Arshtib*a*r*a*,— *spear-bearer.*

Av*a*,— dem. pron., *this, that.* Avest., av*a*; Slav., ova.

Av*a*,— verbal prefix, *from.* Skt., av*a*.

Ava,— *so long.* Correl. to yava.

Av*a*tha,— *thus.*

Av*a*da,— 1) *there*; 2) *thither.*

— In ablative sense with suffix s*a*, *from that place, thence.*

Av*a*p*a*ra,— *thence.*

Av*a*shciy,— *whatever, anything, all.* Av*a*-ciy.

Av*a*h.— *aid, guard.* Avest., avo.

Avah,— denom. from preceding.

— with prefix patiy, *to seek aid.*

Avahyaradiy,—*for this reason, therefore.* Composed of gen. of pron. ava, and loc. of rad.

Avahanam,—*village*; from root vah, to dwell. Skt., vas; Lat., vesta; Germ., woh-nen; AS., wesan; Eng., was.

Asagarta,—*Sagartian.*

Asagartiya,—*Sargartian.*

Asabari, or asbari,—*soldier*; properly, *a horseman.*

Aspacana,—a proper name in Persia. Probably from aspa, horse; according to Herodotus, the name of a man. (For aspa, cf. Meyer in idg. Forsch., p. 329 [1892]).

Asman,—*heaven.* Skt., açman.

Ashnaiy,—*near.*

Azda,—*knowledge.*

Ah,—*to be.* Skt., as; Avest., ah; Lat., es-t; Goth., is-t; Eng., is.

Ahifrastad,—*severe punishment.*

I

I,—*to go.* Skt., I; Avest., I; Lat.. i-re.

— with prefix atiy, *to go beyond, carry farther.*

— with nij, *to go forth.*

— with patiy, *to go against.*

— with para, *to proceed.*

— with apari, *to follow, obey.*

Ida,—*here.* Skt., iha; Avest., idha.

Ima,—pron., *this*. Skt., ima; Avest., ima.

Imani,—name of a man in Susa, who excited a tumult against Darius.

Ish,—*to send*. Skt., ish; Avest., ish.

— with prefix fra, *to send forth*.

Ishu,—*arrow*. Skt., ishu.

Izava,—*tongue*.

U

(H)u,—*good, well*. It occurs only in the beginning of a compound. Skt., su; Avest., hu.

Uta,—*and*. Skt., uta; Avest., uta.

Utana,—name of one of the six who dethroned false Smerdis.

Ud,—verbal prefix. Skt., ud.

Upa,—prefix, *under, to*. Skt., upa; Avest., upa; Lat., sub.

Upa,—prep. with acc., *under*. Cf. above.

Upadara(n)ma,—name of a man in Susiana.

Upariy,—prep. with acc., *above, over*. Skt., upari; Avest., upara; Lat., super; Goth., ufar; Eng., over.

Upasta,—*aid, help*. Upa and sta; cf. Germ., beistand.

(H)ufrasta,—see pars.

(H)ufratu,—*Euphrates*. From u, well; and fra (perhaps a Semitic root), to flow.

(H)ubarta,—see bar.

(H)umartiya,—*possessing good men*.

(H)uvakhshatara,—name of a king c

(H)uv*a*j*a*,— *Susiana.*

(H)uv*a*jiy*a*,— an inhabitant of Susiana.

(H)uv*a*sp*a*,— *possessing good horses.*

(H)uvaip*a*shiy*a*,— *one's own pleasure, independence.* (h)uva, self; Skt., sv*a*; Lat., suus.

Uvad*a*id*a*y*a*,— name of a city in Persia.

(H)uvam*a*rshiyush,— *committing suicide.* (h)uva, self; Skt., sv*a*: and m*a*rsh; Avest., meresh, to die.

(H)uvar*a*z*a*mi or (H)uvar*a*z*a*miy*a*,— *Chorasmia.*

Us,— cf. ud.

Us*a*t*a*shan*a*,— *lofty building, temple.* Us (see above) and t*a*sh; Skt., t*a*ksh; Avest., t*a*sh, to form; Lat., tig-mum.

(H)ushk*a*,— *dry.* Avest., hushka. (Cf. idg. Forschungen, Bartholomae, p. 488 [1892]).

Uz*a*ma,— *cross.*

Uhyam*a*,— name of a castle in Armenia.

K

K*a*,— interrog. pron., *who.* Skt., k*a*; Avest., k*a*; Lat., qui.

— with personal or relative pronoun having an indefinite force: *(who)ever.*

K*a*uf*a*,— *mountain.*

K*a*t*a*p*a*tuk*a*,— *Cappadocia.*

K*a*n,— *to dig, scratch.* Skt., kh*a*n; Avest., k*a*n; Lat., cun-iculus.

— with prefix av*a*, *to throw down with violence, displace.*

— with ni, *to dig down, destroy.*

— with vi, *to destroy.*

K*a*m*a*n*a*,— *desirous, faithful.* Skt., k*a*m, to desire; *few?*

K*a*(m)p*a*d*a*,— name of a province in Media.

K*a*(m)bujiy*a*,— *Cambyses.*

K*a*r,— *to do.* Skt., kṛ; Avest.. k*a*r; Lat., cre-o.

— with prefix p*a*ri, *to guard.*

K*a*shciy,— indef. pron., *whoever.*

— with preceding n*a*iy, *no one.*

K*a*rk*a*,— name of a people.

Kapish*a*kani,— name of a fortress in Arachasia.

Kam*a*,— *wish, desire.* Skt., kam*a*.

Kar*a*,— 1) *people*; 2) *army.* Cf. k*a*r.

Kug*a*n*a*ka,— name of a city in Persia.

Kud(u)ru,— name of a city in eastern Media.

Kuru,— *Cyrus.*

Kushiy*a*,— name of a people.

Kh

Khsh*a*tr*a*— nom. and acc., khsh*a*tr*a*m; *rule, kingdom.* Skt., ksh*a*tr*a*; Avest., khsh*a*thr*a*.

Khsh*a*tr*a*pav*a*n,— nom., khsh*a*tr*a*pava; *satrap.* From khsh*a*tr*a* (cf. above) and pa (to guard, protect).

Khsh*a*thrit*a*,— name of a man who excited a tumult against Darius in Media.

Khsh*a*p*a*,— acc., khsh*a*p*a*; *night.* Skt., ksh*a*p; Avest., khsh*a*p.

Khshay*a*thiy*a*, — *king.* (Cf. Brugmann in Idg. Forschungen, p. 177 [1892]).

Khsh*a*yarsha,— *Xerxes.*

Khshi (?)

— with prefix pati, *to rule, reign*. (It is possible to refer patiy*a*khsh*a*iy to akhsh, see).

Khshnas,— *to know*. (Perhaps connected with Skt., J*n*a; Avest., khshna; Lat., co-gno-sco; Goth., kaun; Germ., kann; Eng., know, can).

G

G*a*itha,— *flock, herd.*

G*a*ub*a*ruv*a*,— *Gobryas*. The name of a man.

G*a*umat*a*,— name of a Magian.

G*a*ush*a*,— acc. dual, g*a*usha; *ear*. Avest., g*a*osh*a*.

G*a*(n)dut*a*v*a*,— name of a country in western Arachosia.

G*a*(n)d*a*r*a*,— name of a country near the Indus.

G*a*m,— *to go*. Skt., g*a*m; Avest., g*a*m; Lat., venio (for guemio ?); Goth., quam; Germ., kommen; Eng., come.

— with prefix a, *to approach, come.*

— with h*a*m, *to gather one's self together.*

— with para, *to depart.*

G*a*rb,— *to seize, take*. Skt., gr*a*bh; Avest., g*a*rep; Germ., greif-en (?); Eng., gripe (?).

G*a*rm*a*p*a*da,— name of a month.

G*a*st*a*,— *revealed, declared*. Skt., g*a*d.

G*a*thu,— 1) *foundation, firm place*; 2) *throne*. Avest., gathu.

Gud,— Skt., guh; Avest., guz.

— with prefix ap*a*, *to conceal.*

Gub,— *to speak*; middle, *to be called* or *named.*

C

Caishpi,— son of Achaemenes.

Cashma,— *eye.*

Ca,— encl., *and.* Skt., ca; Avest., ca; Lat., que.

Ciy,— neut., ciy and cish; *who, what.* Skt., cit; Avest., ci.

— cishciy, *whatever.* (For change of etym. t to sh before c, cf. idg. Forschungen, p. 488 [1891]).

— anivashciy, *some other.*

Ciya(n)karam,— *how many, manifold.*

Cicikhri,— name of a man.

Cita,— *so long as.*

Citra,— *seed, offspring.*

Citra(n)takhma,— name of a man.

J

Jad,— *to supplicate, pray; to grant prayer.*

Jatar,— nom. jata, *enemy.* Cf. jan.

Jan,— *to smite.* Skt., han; Avest., jan.

— with prefix ava, *to smite down, kill.*

— with fra, *to cut off.*

Jiv,— *to live.* Skt., jiv; Avest., jiv; Lat., vivo.

Jiva,— *life.*

T

Taiyiya or maiyiya,— doubtful word (*witness ?*).

Tauma,— *race, family.* Avest., taokhma.

Takabara,— epithet of the Greeks, *wearing crowns, wearing long hair.*

Takhmaspada,— name of one of the commanders of Darius.

Takhs,— *to construct, build.* Skt., taksh; Avest., tash.

— with prefix ham, *to work together, help, work.*

Tacara,— *building, temple.*

Tar,— *to cross, put across.* Skt., tr; Avest., tar; Lat., in-tra-re, trans; Old German, durh; Eng., through.

— with prefix fra, *to go forward.*

— with vi, *to put over* or *across.*

Taradaraya,— *across the sea*; from tara, across, and daraya, the sea.

Tars,— *to tremble, fear.* Skt., tras; Avest., tars-ti.

Tarava,— name of a city in Yutia of Persia.

Tigra,— name of a fortress in Armenia.

Tigra,— *Tigris*; perhaps feminine of an adjective, tigra, sharp. Skt., tij. Cf. Dionys. perig. v. 984, "The Medes call the Tigris an arrow."

Tigrakhauda,— name of a Scythian tribe.

Tuvam,— *thou.* Skt., tvam; Avest., thwam; Lat., tu; Germ., du. (Cf. Wackernagel, über ein Gesetz der idg. Wortstellung, idg. Forsch., p. 403 [1892]).

Tya,— rel. pron., *who, that.* Skt., ya; Avest., hya;

— tyapatiy, *whatever.*

Th

Thaigarci,— name of a month.

Thakata,— *then* (?). (This meaning is a conventional one. A recent theory proposes a widely different signification, but at present both the etymology and interpretation of the word are doubtful).

Thatagush,— name of a people.

Thad,— *to go, err* (?). (Perhaps connected with: Skt., sad; Lat., sideo; Got., sat; Eng., sit).

Thah,— *to say, speak.* Thatiy for Thahatiy.

Thukhra,— name of a Persian.

Thuravahara,— name of a month.

Thard,— *kind, sort, manner.*

Tr

Trar.

— with prefix ni, *to restore.*

Tritiya,— *third.* Skt., tritiya; Avest., thritya; Lat., tertius; Goth., thridya; Eng., third.

D

Daushtar,— *friend.*

Dan,— *to flow.*

Dar,— *to hold, to hold one's self; to delay, halt.* Skt., dhṛ; Avest., dar.

Daraya,— *sea.*

Darsh,— *to dare, subdue.* Skt., dhṛsh; Avest., daresh; Eng., durst.

Darsham,— *strongly, very.*

Darshama,— *insolence, ferocity, violence.*

Dast*a*,—*hand.* Skt., hast*a*; Avest., zast*a*.

D*a*sh*a*bari,—*stretching out the hand, submissive.*

D*a*hyaush,—*region, province.* Skt., d*a*syu; Avest., daqyu.

Da,—*to give.* Skt., da; Avest., da; Lat., da-re.

Da,—*to place, create, do, make.* Skt., dha; Lat., con-do, cre-do; AS., dom; Eng., doom.

Da,—*to know, understand.* Avest., da.

Dat*a*,—*law.* Cf. da.

Dad*a*rshi,—a name of an Armenian and Persian.

Daduhy*a*,—one of the six who, with Darius Hystaspes, deprived false Smerdis of his kingdom.

Dar*ayava*(h)u,—*Darius.* Cf. d*a*r; for second member of the compound, cf. Skt. v*a*su, good; as a noun, wealth: perhaps from v*a*s, to shine (like Eng. splendid). Cf. Lat., us-tus, Ves-uvius; Eng., East.

Dasy*a*man,—*he who stretches forth, serves; an attendant* (perhaps).

Di,—pron. root, *this.* (Cf. Wachernagel, über ein Gesetz der idg. Wortstellung, idg. Forsch., p. 405 [1892]).

Di,—*to see.* Avest., di.

Di,—*to remove, take away.*

Dida,—*castle.*

Dipi,—*letter, inscription.* Perhaps connected with Skt., lip.

Duban*a*,—name of a country in Babylonia.

Dur*a*,—loc. dur*a*iy, dur*a*y, and dur*a*i; *far, distant.* Skt., dur*a*.

Duruj,—*to deceive, be false.* Skt., druh; Avest., druj.

Duruva,—*firm, well, sound, secure.* Skt., dhruva.

Duvaishtam,—*a long time.*

Duvar,—*to make, accomplish* (?).

Duvara,—*door, court.* Skt., dvara; Avest., dvara.

Duvarthi,—*gate.*

Duvitatarnam,—*separately* (?), *for a long time* (?).

Duvitiya,—*second.* Skt., dvitiya; Avest., bitya; Lat., duo, bis; Goth., tvai; AS., twa; Eng., two.

Dushiyara,—*misfortune*; from dush. Skt., dus, ill, and yara; Avest., yare.

Drauga,—*lie, falsehood.* Cf. duruj.

Draujana,—*false, deceiving.*

Dra(n)ga,—*a long time.*

N

Naiba,—*beautiful, pretty.*

Naiy,—*not.*

Naditabira,—name of a man who excited opposition against Darius in Babylon.

Napa,—*grandson.* Skt., napat; Avest., napat; Lat., nepo(t)s; AS., nefa.

Nabukudracara,—name of a Babylonian king.

Nabunita,—name of the last Babylonian king.

Navama,—*ninth.* Skt., navama; Avest., navan; Lat., novem; Goth., niun; AS., nigan; Eng., nine.

Naman,—*name.* Skt., naman; Avest., namąn; Lat., nomen; Goth., namo; Eng., name.

Nau,—*ship.* Skt., naus; Lat., navis.

Naha,—*nose.* Skt., nasa.

Ni,—*to conduct, lead.* Skt., ni.

Nij,—verbal prefix, *from.* Skt., nis; Avest., nish.

Nipad.—loc. nipadiy, *footprint, on foot.* Ni, down (Skt., ni; Lat., in; AS., in), and pad, foot (Skt., pad; Avest., padha; Lat., pe(d)s; Goth., fotus; Eng., foot).

Nisaya,—name of a country in Media.

Nyaka,—*grandfather.* Avest., nyaka.

Nuram,—*now.*

P

Paishiyauvada,—name of a region.

Pat,—*to fall.* Skt., pat; Lat., peto.

— with prefix ud, *to rise up.*

Patiy,—prep. and verbal prefix. 1) *in*; 2) *against*; 3) *throughout.* Often postpositive. Skt., prati; Avest., paiti.

Patikara,—*image, effigy.*

Patigrabana,—name of a city in Parthia.

Patipadam,—*in its own place.* From patiy (cf. above) and pad (cf. nipad).

Patish,—with acc., *towards.* Cf. patiy.

Pathi,—*way, road.* Skt., patha; Avest., panthan; Lat., pon(t)s; Old Germ., pad, fad; AS., padh; Eng., path.

Parauva,—*eastern.*

Paraga,—name of a Persian mountain.

Parana,—*former.*

Para,—prep., postpositive, and verbal prefix, *from, backward.* Skt., para; Lat., per; Goth., fra; Old Germ., fer; Germ., ver; AS., for, as in Eng., forgive.

Pariy,—prep. and verbal prefix, *around, about, concerning.* Skt., pari; Avest., pairi.

Paru,—gen. plur., parunam and paruvnam; *much, many.* Skt., puru; Avest., pouru; Lat., plus; Goth., filu; Germ., viel.

Paruva,—*anterior eastern*; acc. neut., paruvam: *before.* Avest., paourva.

Paruviya,—*before, anterior*; in abl. sense, haca paruviyata. Skt. Ved., purvya; Avest., paourvya.

Paruzana,—gen. plur., paruzananam and paruvzananam; *possessing many kinds of peoples.*

Parthava,—*Parthia.*

Pars,—1) *to ask*; 2) *to inquire about something.* Skt., prach; Avest., pares; Lat., preco; Goth., frah; Germ., fragen.

— with preceding (h)u, *to examine carefully, punish*; part. (h)u-frastam.

— with prefix pati, *to examine, read.*

Pasa,—*after.*

Pasava,—*afterwards, thereafter.* Pasa and ava.

Pa,—*to protect, sustain.* Skt., pa; Avest., pa; Lat., pa-vi, pa-scor.

Patishuvari,—a race inhabiting a portion of Persia.

Parsa,—*Persia, Persian.*

Pitar,—*father*. Skt., pitṛ; Avest., pita; Lat., pater; Goth., fadar; Germ., vater; AS., faeder; Eng., father. Cf. pa.

Pish,—*to scrape, graze*. Skt., pish; Lat., pinso.

— with prefix ni, *to write on*.

Pirava.—*Nile*.

Putiya,—name of a people.

Putra,—*son*. Skt., putra; Avest., puthra; Lat., puer (?).

F

Fra,—verbal prefix. *before, for*. Skt., pra; Avest., fra; Lat., pro; Eng., fore.

Fratama,—*first, leader*.

Framana,—*authority, command, precepts*.

Fravarti,—proper name, *Phraortes*.

Fraharvam,—acc. neut. in adverbial sense, *altogether*. From fra and harva, haruva.

Frada,—name of a ruler in Margia.

B

Baga,—*god*. Skt., bhaga; Avest., bagha; Goth., ga-bigs.

Bagabukhsha,—name of one of those who with Darius dethroned false Smerdis; *Megabyzos*.

Bagabigna,—name of a Persian.

Ba(n)d,—*to bind*, Skt., bandh; Avest., band; Goth., bindan; Eng., bind.

Ba(n)daka,—*subject, servant*.

Bar,—*to bear, sustain, protect.* Skt., bhṛ; Avest., bar; Lat., fero; Goth., bairan; AS., beran; Eng., bear.

— with prefix pati, *to bring back, replace, restore.*

— with para, *to bear away.*

— with fra, *to carry off, assign.*

Bardiya,—name of the brother of Cambyses, *Smerdis.*

Bakhtri,—*Bactria.*

Bagayadi,—name of a month.

Baji,—*tribute*; from root baj. Skt., bhaj, to allot.

Babiru,—*Babylon.*

Babiruviya,—*Babylonian.*

Bu,—*to be.* Skt., bhu; Avest., bu; Lat., fuo, fui, perhaps bam (in amabam); AS., beom; Germ., bin; Eng , be.

Bumi,—*ground, earth.* Skt., bhumi; Avest., bumi.

Bratar,—*brother.* Skt., bhratṛ; Avest., bratar; Lat., frater; Goth., brothar; AS., brodher; Eng., brother.

M

Maka,—name of a people.

Magu,—*Magian*, a Median people from whom the priests were elected.

Maciya,—name of a people.

Mathiśhta,—*the greatest, leader.*

Man,—*to think. ponder.* Skt., man; Avest., man; Lat., mens; Germ., meinen.

Man,—*to remain.* Avest., man; Lat., maneo.

Mar,—*to die*. Skt., mṛ; Avest., mar; Lat., morior; AS., mordh.

Margu,—name of a region east and north of Areia.

Martiya,—1) *mortal, man*; cf. mar above. 2) name of a man who excited a tumult against Darius. In P. the gen. sing. is contracted to martihya.

Marduniya,—name of a man, *Mardonius*.

Ma,—*to measure*. Skt., ma; Avest., ma; Lat., meto.

— with prefix a, past part., amata, *tested, tried, prolonged*.

Ma,—prohibitive particle, *not*. Skt., ma; Avest., ma.

Matya,—*that not, lest*.

Mada,—*Median, Media*.

Maniya,—*place of remaining, dwelling*. Cf. man.

Margaya or Margava,—*Margianian*.

Maha,—*month*; contracted gen. mahya. Skt., masa; Lat., mensis; AS., mona; Eng., month.

M(i)thra,—name of a Persian God.

Mudraya,—*Egypt*; nom. plur., *Egyptians*.

Y

Yauna,—*Ionian, Ionia*. Skt., Yavana.

Yatha,—1) *as, when*; 2) *because*; 3) *in order that, that*. From rel. root, ya.

Yada,—*duty*.

Yadiy,—1) *if*; 2) *when*. Skt., yadi; Avest., yedhi.

— with padiy, *if perchance*.

Yanaiy,—(?)

Yata,—1) *during, while*; 2) *until.* From rel. root, ***ya.***

Yan*a*,—*favor.* Avest., yan*a*.

Yava,—*as long as.* Skt., yav*a*t.

Yutiya,—name of a region in Persia.

Yuviya,—*canal.*

R

R*a*uc*a*,—acc. sing., r*a*uc*a*; *day.* Connected with Skt., ruc, to shine; Lat., luceo; AS., leoht; Eng., light.

R*a*ut*a*,—*river.*

R*a*kha,—name of a city in Persia.

R*a*ga,—name of a district in Media.

R*a*d (?),—Skt., r*a*h.

— with prefix av*a*, *to relinquish, leave.*

R*a*s,—*to come.* Desiderative: cf. Brugmann in idg. Forsch., p. 173 (1892).

— with prefix para, *to arrive.*

— with prefix ni, *to descend.*

Rad,—*joy, delight.*

— loc. sing., radiy with gen., *for the sake of.*

— av*a*hyaradiy, *for the sake of this thing, for this reason.*

Rast*a*,—*right.*

V

V*a*in,—*to see, behold.* The middle is used in the passive sense. Avest., vaen.

V*a*umis*a*,—name of a Persian.

Vaj,— *to lead.* Skt., vah; Avest., vaz; AS., wegan.

Vayaspara,— name of a Persian.

Var,— *to declare, make (one) believe, convince.*

Varkana,— *Hyrcania.*

Vardana,— nom. sing., vardanam, *fortified town, city, state.* Connected with Skt. vṛdh, to increase; Avest., va-red; AS., waldan, weald.

Vasiy,— *much, very, greatly.* (Possibly connected with Greek *ἑκών,* "nach Wunsch". Bartholomae).

Vashna,— *desire, power, grace.* Cf. vas, to desire.

Vazraka,— *great.*

Vahyazdata,— name of a man who excited a tumult against Darius Hystaspes.

Vahauka,— name of a Persian.

Va,— enclitic particle, *or.* Skt., va; Lat., ve.

Vith,— 1) *clan*; 2) *race, fellow.*

Vithiya,— *pertaining to the same race.*

Vithin (?),— *possessing the same race.* The instr. plur. vithibish, which alone justifies the supposition of the existence of this adjective, I have explained in grammar (86, c) as from noun vith.

Vida,— (?)

Vidarna,— name of a Persian.

Vi(n)dafra,— name of a Mede.

Vi(n)dafrana,— name of a Persian.

Viyakhna,— name of a month.

Viyatarayam,— see tar.

Vivana,— name of a Persian.

Visa,—*all, every.* Skt., viçva.

Visadahyu,—acc. sing. masc. visadahyum, *possessing all provinces.*

Vispazana,—gen. plur. masc. vispazanam, *possessing all kinds of peoples.*

Vishtaspa,—*Hystaspes*, the father of Darius.

S

Saka,—*Scythian, Scythia.*

Saku(n)ka,—name of a man who excited opposition among the Sakae against Darius Hystaspes.

San,—(?)

— with prefix vi, *to destroy.*

Sar,—*to kill.* (?)

Sikayauvati,—name of a fortress in Media.

Suguda,—*Sogdiana.*

Skudra,—name of a people.

Star,—*to sin.* (?)

Sta,—*to stand.* Skt., stha; Avest., sta; Lat., sta-re; AS., standan; Eng., stand.

— with prefix ava (caus.), *to establish, constitute.*

— with ni (caus.), *to enjoin, command.*

Stana,—*place.*

Sparda,—name of a people.

Sh

Sha and Shi,—stem of a pron. encl., 3 pers. Skt., sa; Avest., he. (Cf. Wackernagel, uber ein Gesetz der idg. Wortstellung, idg. Forsch., p. 404 [1892]).

Sharastibara,—*bow-bearer*. or perhaps for arshtibara, *spear-bearer.*

Shiyati,—*spirit, intelligence, wisdom.* (?) (shayatim, P.)

Shiyu,—*to go, set out.*

Shuguda,— see Suguda.

Z

Zara(n)ka,— *Drangiana.*

Zazana,— name of a fortified town near Babylon

Zura,—*power.*

Zurakara,—*despot.* From zura (see above) and kara (see kar).

H

Haina.—*army.* Skt., sena; Avest., haena.

Hauv,—*this.* Skt., a-sau; Avest. hau.

Hakhamani,—*Achaemenes*, originator of the race of the Achaemenides.

Hakhamanishiya,—*of the race of Achaemenides.*

Hangmatana,—*Ecbatana*; leading city of Media, at the foot of the mountains of Alvend. From ham (together), and gam (to go).

Haca,—prep with ablative, *from.* Avest., haca.

Ha(n)j,—*to draw throw*

— with fra, *to throw forth.*

Had,—*to sit.* Skt., sad; Avest., had; Lat., sedeo; AS., sittan; Eng., sit

— witn prefix ni (caus.), *to constitute, establish.*

H*a*da,— prep with instrumental, *with* Skt., s*a*h*a*, Avest., hadh*a*.

H*a*dish,—*place, dwelling, royal seat, palace.* Cf. h*a*d

H*a*(n)duga,—*edict.*

H*a*ndit*a*,— name of a Babylonian

H*a*m,— verbal prefix, *together with.* Skt., s*a*m Avest., h*a*m.

H*a*ma,—*together, all.* Skt., s*a*m*a*; Avest., h*a*m*a* Lat., simul; Goth., sama; Germ., zusammen, AS., same

H*a*m*a*pit*a*r,—*having a common father.* From h*a*m*a* and pit*a*r.

H*a*m*a*r*a*,—*war.* Skt., s*a*m*a*r*a*

H*a*m*a*r*a*n*a*,— nom. and acc. sing., h*a*m*a*r*a*n*a*m; *conflict, battle.*

H*a*mat*a*r,—*having a common mother.* From h*a*m and m*a*t*a*r. Skt., matṛ; Lat., mater; Eng., mother. Cf. ma.

H*a*mitriy*a*,—*rebellious.*

H*a*r*a*iv*a*,— name of a country, *Area.*

H*a*r*a*uv*a*ti,— loc. H*a*r*a*uv*a*t*a*iya, *Arachosia.*

H*a*ruv*a*,—*all, every.* Skt., s*a*rv*a*; Avest., h*a*ruv*a*: Lat., salvus.

H*a*shitiy*a*,—*rebellious.*

H*a*shiy*a*,— neut. h*a*shĭy*a*m, *true.*

Hin(d)u,—*India*; region near the river Indus. Skt., sindhu; Avest., hindu.

Hum*a*v*a*rk*a*,—appellation of the race of the Scythians.

Hyap*a*r*a*,— acc. in adverbial sense; also with patiy, *again.* From hy*a* and ap*a*r*a*.

Lightning Source UK Ltd.
Milton Keynes UK
UKOW041820040112

184747UK00005B/34/P

9 781241 073060